RUSTING OUT, BURNING OUT, BOWING OUT

STRESS AND SURVIVAL ON THE JOB

Dr. John Howard, Dr. David Cunningham, Dr. Peter Rechnitzer

A Financial Post/Macmillan Book

Reprinted 1979

ISBN 0-88896-077-8

Printed and bound in Canada

Financial Post Books,
481 University Ave.,
Toronto, Ont. M5W 1A7

The Macmillan Company of Canada,
70 Bond St.,
Toronto, Ont. M5B 1X3

The authors, all associates at the University of Western Ontario, have been studying the causes and effects of stress and stress-induced illness, particular among managers, for the last half-decade.

John H. Howard, D.B.A., is an associate professor in the School of Business Administration. His areas of interest include work and career problems among managers and professionals, particularly as they relate to stress, performance and satisfaction.

David A. Cunningham, Ph.D., is a professor in the Faculties of Medicine and Physical Education, where his work involves coronary heart disease and physical activity.

Peter A. Rechnitzer, M.D., F.R.C.P.(C), F.R.C.P.(E.), is a clinical professor of medicine. His special interest lies in the area of cardiac rehabilitation.

Contents

Contents

Acknowledgments

THIS BOOK can be seen in part as an interim report on our research into the problems of stress among managerial and professional people. Our research continues, and we expect over the next few years to add more knowledge to what's here.

We've tried to make the book interesting, informative and practical, sparing the reader academic jargon and statistical analysis. To keep it *useful* for the practising manager has been one of our prime goals.

We are, of course, indebted to many. The Plan for Excellence at the School of Business Administration, University of Western Ontario, has funded most of our work. Many Canadian corporations contribute to this fund, and we thank them for their support. We would also like to thank Doreen Sanders, editor of the Business Quarterly, published by Western's business school. Over the years Doreen has published many of our articles, and she's a constant source of encouragement.

Our research subjects, who remain anonymous, have always given willingly and enthusiastically of their support. From them we've both asked much and learned much—and they've always been willing to help.

Many colleagues also have provided ideas, encouragement and the opportunity to pursue this work. With three authors representing three different faculties, there are so many in this

9

category that we can convey our gratitude here only in general terms.

Two individuals do, however, require special recognition. Lili Vlach and Pat McCabe have been of continuing assistance to us through the years. Lili has directed most of the laboratory testing often required in our research. Pat has insured that many administrative and secretarial duties have been done with dispatch. Their work is always outstanding, and we thank them very much.

One other individual deserves special recognition. Dr. Hans Selye, who graciously wrote the foreword for our book, has been the pioneer in the field of stress. The work he started and sustained over the years has been an inspiration to many. He continues to provide encouragement and support to researchers from around the world at his International Institute of Stress in Montreal.

While many have helped, the work and responsibility remain our own.

J.H.H.
D.A.C.
P.A.R.

Foreword

SINCE it was I who wrote the first scientific article on stress, way back in 1936, it has become a tradition for various people to ask me for introductions and forewords, and I must say that I write some of them with considerable hesitation. But this one does not fall into that category.

I do not know all the authors of this book equally well, but I do know John H. Howard; also, I have heard him lecture and have read his manuscripts and papers for quite some time. Rarely have I encountered anybody whose main schooling is in business administration but who nevertheless knows so much about medicine and the biophysical machinery to detect stress, its neurohormonal manifestations and virtually every other aspect of the field.

I think the best way to add my little bit to this volume by way of a foreword would be to give a brief résumé of what, after four decades of clinical and laboratory research, I consider the most important principles of behavior for handling stress:

1. **Find your own stress level**—the speed at which you can run toward your chosen goal. Make sure that both the stress level and the goal are really your own, and are not imposed by society, for only you can know what you want and how fast you can accomplish it. There is no point in forcing a turtle to run like a racehorse or in preventing a

racehorse from running faster than a turtle because of some "moral obligation." The same is true of people.

2. **Be an altruistic egoist.** Do not try to suppress the natural instinct of all living beings to look after themselves first. Yet the wish to be of some use, to do some good to others, is also natural; we are social beings, and everybody wants somehow to earn respect and gratitude. Both these natural desires are served by my injunction: Be necessary! If you obey it, it gives you the greatest degree of safety, because no one wishes to destroy a person who is useful; in fact, he will inspire love in his neighbors—which brings me to my final principle.

3. **Earn thy neighbor's love.** This is a contemporary modification of the maxim "Love thy neighbor as thyself." It recognizes that not all men are lovable and that it is impossible to love on command.

Perhaps two short lines can summarize what I have discovered from all my thought and research:

Fight for *your* highest *attainable* aim,
but do not put up resistance in vain.

I think everybody can see that since this is my position, I would enthusiastically endorse the book by Howard, Cunningham and Rechnitzer. They look at the subject from points of view completely different from my own, but come to essentially the same conclusion.

In my opinion, this volume should be present not only in libraries, but on the desks of all those who do not know how to manage stress, and consequently suffer from it instead of benefiting. I certainly want to express my appreciation both to the authors and to the publisher for creating this remarkable work.

Hans Selye, C.C., M.D., Ph.D., D.Sc.
President, International Institute of Stress
University of Montreal
Nov. 30, 1978

1. Stress in your life

About its patterns and causes on the job

IN THE tense days of the Watergate aftermath, as the world waited for the finale, an astute journalist noted that Richard Nixon mightn't be able to finish his second term, even though neither impeachment nor resignation seemed likely at that time.

What seemed more probable, however, was mental or physical breakdown—the result of the enormous pressures of the presidency and the terrible reality of the Watergate tragedy.

The writer, William C. Heine of the London (Ontario) Free Press, noted evidence that Nixon was nearing his capacity to cope with stress. First, there was the deterioration in his physical appearance. In the previous six months he seemed to have acquired a harried, worried look that contrasted sharply with the self-confident, relatively placid appearance he'd made during his second inaugural.

Then there was his bout with virus pneumonia. He went into the hospital without anyone seeing him go, was there about a week, during which he was seen by few if any people other than his immediate family. And then he emerged to continue with business. The circumstances of his entry into hospital and his return to the White House suggested that while pneumonia may have existed, a collapse due to physical and emotional stress was at least possible.

A third incident had occurred in New Orleans. The tension

and stress were particularly visible in the rough, rude way the President had grabbed his press secretary, spun him on his heel, and literally pushed him toward the press corps.

The evidence, of course, was only suggestive, but the signals of excessive stress were classic:

A change in appearance.
A change in normal attitudes and behavior.
And the development of minor illnesses.

Stress, of course, isn't peculiar to those in high political office. Many employees in the middle ranks of business and industry have had similar experiences. In fact, there are good reasons why managers at all levels should be aware of and very concerned about the phenomenon called stress.

To see why, first of all, we need only to observe the results of the so-called "executive monkey" experiments, which portrayed clearly the stressful aspects of responsibility and decision making. These experiments used four pairs of rhesus monkeys in a "behavioral-stress" situation. In each pair of monkeys, one animal was designated the experimental animal and the other the control animal.

During the experiments, both monkeys in each pair were exposed to an electric shock, but only the experimental animal could learn to avoid the shock by pressing a lever at specific intervals. The lever was not available to the control animal. If the lever was pressed in time, no shock was administered to either the experimental animal or the control animal. Thus, both animals were shocked an equal number of times, but only the experimental animal could determine whether or not the shock would occur.

After a few weeks the experimental animal in all four pairs died from gastrointestinal ulcerations. The control animals, which had received the same amount of electric shock but were not faced with the decision that controlled it, all lived. And no ulcers were found.

These experiments tend to convey the possibility for extreme stress when a human being takes on the responsibility for making decisions on important issues. In real life, of course, we often compound the situation by assigning the responsibility while at the same time limiting the power needed to fulfill the obligation.

In fact, while the "executive monkey" experiment tends to convey the stress aspects of responsibility, the issue is not that clear. It could be argued, for example, that if the experimental animal had indeed *learned* to control the shock, then neither animal would have suffered. Most research shows that it is not responsibility per se that is stress-producing, but it's responsibility without power to influence outcomes that has the greatest stress potential. In short, it's the sense of "helplessness" that's debilitating.

A Swedish experiment made the point graphically. It measured a number of physiological indicators (heart rate and so forth) of naval pilots and their navigators as they landed their jet aircraft on a carrier under adverse weather conditions. In this situation, while both individuals shared the same stressful situation, only the pilot had control. But in every case the navigator experienced the greatest stress.

Being in control in a stressful situation and having the capacity to influence it has great therapeutic value. In contrast, the navigator's sense of helplessness produced the greater stress reaction.

Numerous other experiments and day-to-day experiences make the same point. How do you feel when you're riding as a passenger in your own car and someone else (particularly your spouse!) is driving? It's usually not the driving conditions that produce the stress, but your sense of helplessness in not being in control. The feeling is universal and it has many sources in our lives.

If at work you have responsibility for making decisions (with or without enough power to see them through), then this book is for you ... because, no matter what your level in the organization, stress may be the most significant threat to your staying effective in your job.

The first major problem in your career was to *become* an effective manager. Now, the second is to *maintain* that effectiveness. Stress and the maintenance of your effectiveness is a key issue facing both you and your organization.

Stress, of course, isn't new to managers, but we now have new

17

reasons to be worried about it.

First, there's the issue of change.

Change Sickness

In work at the University of Washington, researchers found that if we experience enough change in our life we increase the probability of illness and disease. They compiled a list of 43 common life events. Each event was ranked as to the relative amount of adjustment required to cope with these events. The events were weighted and points assigned to each event. The questionnaire is reproduced opposite.

The number of events, and consequently the number of points, an individual accumulated in a period of time turned out to be a significant predictor of both the onset of illness and the severity of illness. The more points the individual scored on the life-change scale, the more serious was the disease he was likely to develop. The high-risk groups were those who scored more than 300 points in a 12-month period. The illnesses were found to occur sometime in the year following the accumulation of the points.

Several aspects of the study are worth noting. In the first place, the study confirmed that ordinary life events, whether they can be controlled or not, carry a significant stress burden. If the events in our life require change and adaptation, then the experience carries some burden of stress.

In the second place, the accumulation of enough stress events over a period of time increases the probability of illness and disease—and the more stress events we accumulate, the more serious the illness is likely to be.

The third point the study seems to confirm is that experiences we might consider to be enjoyable, but that require some adaptation, still carry with them a burden of stress. It seems likely, however, that unenjoyable and unexpected experiences would, in general, be more stress-producing.

In summing up their findings the researchers drew the following conclusions:

"The research showed that human beings do indeed get sick when they have to cope with many of the events of normal life.

Stress, change and sickness

If any of these life events have happened to you in the last 12 months, check Happened column and enter Value in Your Score column.

Item No.	Life event	Happened	Item Value	Your Score
1	Death of spouse		100	
2	Divorce		73	
3	Marital separation		65	
4	Jail term		63	
5	Death of close family member		63	
6	Personal injury or illness		53	
7	Marriage		50	
8	Fired at work		47	
9	Marital reconciliation		45	
10	Retirement		45	
11	Change in health of family member		44	
12	Pregnancy		40	
13	Sex difficulties		39	
14	Gain of new family member		39	
15	Business readjustment		39	
16	Change in financial state		38	
17	Death of close friend		37	
18	Change to different line of work		36	
19	Change in number of arguments with spouse		35	
20	Mortgage over $10,000		31	
21	Foreclosure of mortgage or loan		30	
22	Change in responsibilities at work		29	
23	Son or daughter leaving home		29	
24	Trouble with in-laws		29	
25	Outstanding personal achievement		28	
26	Wife begins or stops work		26	
27	Begin or end school		26	
28	Change in living conditions		25	
29	Revision of personal habits		24	
30	Trouble with boss		23	
31	Change in work hours or conditions		20	
32	Change in residence		20	
33	Change in schools		20	
34	Change in recreation		19	
35	Change in church activities		19	
36	Change in social activities		18	
37	Mortgage or loan less than $10,000		17	
38	Change in sleeping habits		16	
39	Change in number of family get-togethers		15	
40	Change in eating habits		15	
41	Vacation		13	
42	Christmas		12	
43	Minor violations of the law		11	

Total score for 12 months _____

Note: The more change you have, the more likely you are to get sick. Of those people with over 300 Life Change Units for the past year, almost 90% get sick in the near future; with 150 to 299 Life Change Units, about 50% get sick in the near future; and with less than 150 Life Change Units, only about 30% get sick in the near future.

When they struggle with overwhelming life crisis, they tend to get more-serious diseases. The explanation, we suspect, is that the activity of coping can lower resistance to disease, particularly when one's coping techniques are faulty, when they lack relevance to the type of problems to be solved. This approach to illness is a lesson in human finitude. It reminds us that we have only so much energy, no more. If it takes too much effort to cope with the environment, we have less to spare for preventing disease. When life is too hectic, and when coping attempts fail, illness is the unhappy result."

Stress and change go together. The amount of change in all our lives has been increasing, but it's important to emphasize that managers tend to be at the cutting edge of change in our society. Over the past few years, organizations have been responding continuously to a kaleidoscopic world. They've been adjusting, adapting, attempting to find new structures and new policies to meet changing constraints and opportunities. The need to adapt means stress.

And when organizations are under stress, managers are under stress.

Furthermore, we should now be deeply concerned about stress because the nature of disease and disorder in our society has changed during the past 50 years. The health sciences have largely shrunk the role of plagues and epidemics as killers and cripplers. Chronic diseases are now the main contributors to death and disability.

And each day new evidence, like that above, reveals the relationship of stress to chronic disease.

Another factor is that management jobs have become more complex, more difficult—the result of global change. This can only mean more uncertainty and ambiguity in the future. It also means adjustment, adaptation—and stress.

Uncertainty sickness

Job pressure doesn't necessarily cause stress, contrary to general belief. But conflict and ambiguity do, and we'll look more closely at this later. Uncertainty in our lives also must be cited as a prime cause.

Uncertainty stems from situations over which we have little or no influence, either as to the timing or the outcome of important events.

Recent research on managers in Canadian organizations has revealed the critical role of uncertainty. This work found that job dissatisfaction and stress symptoms were related: the higher the dissatisfaction with job or career, the more the symptoms. In addition, the following five factors, listed in order of importance, were found to be the most significant as contributors to stress and dissatisfaction:

1. A lack of awareness with regard to the opportunities for advancement and promotion.
2. A lack of awareness with regard to how performance is evaluated.
3. A feeling that the job interferes unduly with the individual's personal life.
4. A feeling that the individual lacks the authority and influence needed to carry out assigned responsibilities.
5. Too heavy a workload.

The first two items, the most important, strongly reflect the issue of uncertainty. They're also issues over which management has control; they reflect policies or the lack of policies within the organization.

The feeling that the job interferes with the individual's personal life and the bearing of too heavy a workload likely represent extra hours spent on the job. In the case of managers it's often difficult to judge whether they're simply living up to expectations or following self-imposed work habits, but in either case the outcome is increased stress.

The lack of authority to match responsibilities is an age-old complaint of managers, but it reflects a central issue in terms of stress. This is the issue of influence: a feeling of being able to influence the events that have meaning and importance to the individual. Being without the feeling that you have some control over the important events in your job and career can only lead to stress and the development of stress symptoms.

Uncertainty has always had a significant effect on the emotional and physical health of the individual, but for two principal reasons its psychological importance seems to be increasing. In the first place, as we've seen, change seems to have created more, not less, uncertainty in life.

Combined with the resulting strains on family life, these factors make man's adaptation to the maintenance of the delicate balance between biological and psychological forces an ever-growing burden. This view is strongly supported by Alvin Toffler in his book *Future Shock*.

The second reason why uncertainty is increasing in importance is because the means and institutions people traditionally had used to help cope with uncertainty have either begun to disintegrate or have lost much of their value as effective psychological support. The family and religion are two of the most important institutions that fit in this category. And, while their importance has often been downgraded, little new has come along to prove its effectiveness in supporting the individual during times of uncertainty.

It's somewhat ironic that in a period of increasing uncertainty we're losing our traditional means of coping with the stress involved.

For both managers and organizations, then, the issue of stress has many dimensions. The most evident is simply health and longevity. The personal tragedy in premature death is starkly obvious. The corporate loss is also significant. How many cases have there been where managers, having just risen to the point of assuming key positions, die of coronary heart disease? Is the "bench strength" dying just on the brink of making its most significant contributions? Shouldn't one nurture and be vigilant of such a valuable resource? This is an issue every manager and every corporation should consider.

Do you and your fellow managers have annual medicals? Do you know what you should about alcoholism, nutrition, exercise and stress—in short, how to survive in the 20th century?

What is stress?

The word stress is a much maligned and very imprecise term. In fact, as Prof. Manfred Kets de Vries of McGill University wrote in a recent technical paper, stress is often "used as a

22

'catch-all' term including mental illness, anxiety, tension, fear, ego threat, arousal, and other forms of discomfort," depending on which branch of science happens to be studying it.

Stress, Kets de Vries pointed out, was originally an engineering term, introduced into the social sciences by Hans Selye in 1936. Selye defined stress as "non-specifically induced changes within a biological system." By non-specific, he meant any adaptation to a problem faced by the body, regardless of the nature of the problem. Using this broad definition, the only thing that seems to count is the *intensity* of the demand for readjustment. Selye called the totality of these changes the General Adaptation Syndrome, which has become a very useful concept to describe what happens to your body under stress.

Your reaction to stress occurs in three major stages, according to Selye:

1. The alarm reaction. This includes an initial shock phase during which resistance is lowered, and a counter-shock phase during which your body's defenses are mobilized.
2. The resistance stage. During this stage the bodily signs of the alarm reaction disappear and your body makes its mightiest efforts to adapt. If the stressors persist or the defences prove to be inadequate, your adaptation energy will be depleted and you will reach . . .
3. The stage of exhaustion. The signs of the alarm reaction will re-appear, but in this instance *irreversibly*, because the adaptive mechanisms have collapsed. This stage will end in illness, disease and possibly death.

Selye compares adaptation energy to a bank account from which you can make withdrawals but into which you cannot make deposits. When an organism exhausts the supply of adaptation energy, it will die. Furthermore, your true age will depend on the rate of wear and tear—on your prudence in making withdrawals from this symbolic bank account.

In short, the intensity of your lifestyle will determine whether your physiological or chronological age predominates. Are you "growing old before your time"?

In far simpler terms, stress is probably best understood as a set of physiological responses that our body makes to conditions it finds disturbing. Some of these responses, such as sweaty palms and shaking hands, are highly visible. And we become acutely aware of both the disturbance we're experiencing and at least part of our physiological reaction to it.

At other times our body responds to situations it considers to be stressful, but we're either unaware or insensitive to these reactions. Our stomach may be tightening and our pulse quickening, but we drive on with oblivious persistency toward our objectives.

In general, the disturbances we experience as stressful tend to pass rather quickly. In addition, some types of experiences are more stressful than others, and the same experience can be more or less stressful depending on the individual. Except perhaps at a very general level, the stress potential of a situation depends on *both* the situation and the individual.

Unfortunately, however, as Selye told us, the effects of stress tend to be cumulative. As we live each day and encounter each new stressful experience, there's a residual effect of the experience that accumulates. In a sense, this represents the everyday wear and tear of living.

It serves to remind us that our bodily resources are not infinite —that there are limits to our endowment of physiological resources and that we use them at a slower or faster pace as a matter of choice.

Of course, not all the stress in our life can be controlled. Stress is a ubiquitous experience. Some of the stress we encounter is unexpected and beyond our control. The remainder, however, stems from events about which we make daily decisions. During most of our life the controllable experiences predominate, but the total stress in our life is the sum of these two kinds of experiences. Because each of us has a limited capacity, we become candidates for illness and disease.

The evidence linking excessive stress and chronic disorders such as ulcers, hypertension and heart disease has been steadily growing. But precisely why a particular individual develops a particular disorder is still something of a mystery.

Stress, of course, isn't the only factor responsible. It's difficult, if not impossible, to determine all the causes of a particular disease. There are usually many causes. In any disease, however, some factors are more important than others, and scientists are beginning to find that stress has more and more importance to our overall health.

Stress disorders tend to be basically psychosomatic, in that they operate through our emotions and feelings. Germs and viruses tend not to be involved in these types of disorders. And, fascinatingly, the older concept of illness as being basically the result of disharmony between the individual and his environment is taking on increasing importance.

Most managers understand stress intuitively. It's usually an emotional discomfort accompanied by feelings of not being able to cope—that things are falling apart, that one isn't in control, or just a general unease that all is not well, without any particular cause being apparent. Physically, you feel it in loss of appetite, sleeplessness, sweating, ulcers and other illnesses of varying degress.

Very generally, stress results from the body's preparing itself for activity without the activity following. We could say that the body prepares itself for fight or flight, but neither is possible. Consequently the body's systems are thrown out of balance: excess acid in the stomach, adrenaline in the blood, higher heart rates and other inappropriate reactions. It's that chronic physiological preparation for action, without the action, that leads to disease and disorder.

You could encounter potential stressors almost anywhere, as we've noted, but in organizations particularly, whether large or small, you may be exposed daily to experiences that can lead to intense feelings and emotions. It's true that the stress potential of any of these experiences depends on the individual as well as the situation, but we now can see some general stress patterns in organizations.

Some individual stress patterns

In a recent stress study on more than 2,000 management and professional people in a single organization in Canada, researchers developed five basic stress-symptom patterns. Each pattern was composed of a number of symptoms, each of them a typical

25

reaction to stress:

1. Emotional distress: including insomnia, fatigue, loss of appetite, moodiness and depression.
2. Medication use: including taking of sleeping pills, diet drugs, pain relievers, vitamin pills and tranquilizers.
3. Cardiovascular symptoms: including high blood pressure, rapid heart beat and heart disease.
4. Gastrointestinal symptoms: including ulcers, colitis, digestion problems, diarrhea and nausea.
5. Allergy-respiratory symptoms: including allergies such as hay fever, skin problems such as eczema and psoriasis, and a number of respiratory problems.

Each of these patterns represents a typical way in which people react to stress-producing experiences. But it's not entirely clear why people react to stress in different ways, but factors such as age, sex, culture and education seem to be strongly related to the symptoms an individual is likely to develop.

For example, emotional distress seemed to be particularly high among the young, while medication use and cardiovascular symptoms were found to be more common among older individuals. Gastrointestinal problems and allergy-respiratory problems didn't seem to be age-related. More women than men fell into the categories of emotional distress, medication use, and allergy-respiratory symptoms, but in cardiovascular symptoms it was vice versa.

The study included a large group of French Canadians as well as English-speaking Canadians. And it was found that the francophones were higher than the anglophones in emotional distress and medication use, while the anglophones were higher in gastrointestinal and cardiovascular disorders.

The study associated higher levels of education with medication use, gastrointestinal symptoms and allergy-respiratory symptoms. It related lower levels of education with emotional distress and cardiovascular disease.

These types of symptom patterns indicate that social and cultural tradition determine in part how individuals respond to stress. Consider, for example, the *visibility* of symptoms. The findings indicate that French Canadians react to stress in a more visible way. In other words, the symptoms they develop are highly visible to the outside world. The English-speaking Canadians, on the other hand, are repressors. They turn the stress they experience inward, and consequently the symptoms they develop tend to be associated with the gastrointestinal and cardiovascular systems. The phenomenon of the "stiff upper lip" seems to prevail across their total physical reaction.

Men as compared to women also tend to be repressors. Furthermore, the higher-educated as compared to the lower-educated seem to handle the stress they experience in a less visible way.

These are just a few of the patterns that seem to be associated with stress. There are, of course, other patterns of stress related to the organization itself—particularly as they affect issues of job and career.

Organization stress patterns

There are many jobs and careers characterized by stress levels the incumbents are simply expected to endure. In industry, the job of the foreman has long been recognized as an ideal example of a situation with considerable conflict and ambiguity.

The foreman has been described as the "master and victim of doubletalk" and "the man in the middle"—a position in which, on the one hand, he's expected to identify with and represent the workers' point of view, and on the other, to be responsible to management. It's interesting that associated with the dual and conflicting loyalty of this kind of role is a rather high incidence of ulcers. Foremen are found to have more ulcers than either the workers below them or management above them.

We find similar roles throughout organization life. The salesman's job is another example. Here the individual is caught between his customers' demands and his organization's willingness to respond. In general, in these types of roles or situations the individual experiences the simultaneous occurrence of two or more sets of pressures such that compliance with one makes compliance with the other more difficult.

The level of responsibility in a job is another factor that has considerable consequence in terms of stress. Interestingly, most research on corporate organizations finds that the top jobs are less stressful.

In short, the further up the hierarchy you are, the less stress there seems to be.

It's fascinating to speculate on why such a hierarchial effect might occur—why one's position in the hierarchy is related to health.

First, it's possible that the jobs at the top are less stressful. Such a hypothesis, of course, contradicts much of the mythology concerning the heavy responsibilities of top management.

A second hypothesis would be that the reason there's less stress at the top is that the capacity to cope with stress is one of the qualities taken into account when an individual is promoted up the hierarchy. Consequently, the people at or near the top are those best able to cope with stress.

A third hypothesis would explain the hierarchial differences in terms of a "settling-in" effect. Those at or near the top of the hierarchy have satisfied their ambition and mobility aspirations and have, in a sense, "settled-in." This state of being "settled-in" may, in fact, be associated with less stress.

Probably the best explanation, however, has to do with the power and influence associated with jobs at or near "the top" of the hierarchy. In these jobs, the capacity to influence the sources of stress, rather than simply adjust to it, is considerably greater. In contrast, the person at lower levels in the organization has to do most of the adjusting, most of the coping, himself. He or she has limited capacity to redistribute or influence the sources of stress in the job.

It's important to note that the capacity to influence the variables important to the individual's job and career has great therapeutic value in terms of stress.

The explanation for the hierarchial differences in stress probably encompasses elements of all these explanations. Remember that each of them likely contributes to or detracts from the individual's self-image and thus his self-esteem. A positive self-image is likely to be related to good physical health. A sense of failure and feelings of helplessness have the physiological consequences of higher symptoms and perhaps reduced longevity.

In addition to these factors, research has found others to be

28

significantly related to stress symptoms among managers.

Geographic moves

More stress was reported by those managers who had made one or more geographic moves in the previous five years.

At one time, geographic mobility was a plain fact of managerial life. Companies with widely dispersed operations traditionally relied on the willingness of their managers to move. As promotions became available or problems arose, they took it for granted that a manager would gladly uproot himself and his family to take advantage of the career opportunity. In short, they created a class of managerial gypsies to solve the corporate staffing problems.

This situation appears to be changing. Studies suggest that managers are becoming more and more reluctant to accept transfers within the company. The situation may have reached the point where between a third and a half of all managers would prefer to stay in their present geographic location.

One recent study, conducted with one of the largest companies in Canada, certainly confirms this trend. In this study, fully 48% of the managers and supervisors surveyed indicated they were unwilling to move from their current locations. The illustrations on pages 30-31 compare the attitudes and profiles of those managers.

The attitudes stem, of course, from very different sources. For instance, managers willing to relocate may do so to move to a promising career opportunity. On the other hand, willingness to move may indicate only a desire to escape from an unpleasant job situation. Similarly, managers may want to remain in their current location because they're extremely satisfied with their work and family life, or because they fear moving due to economic reasons.

The important point here is that the study brings out a clear relationship between job dissatisfaction, ambition and mobility—all three of which appear to be closely linked with stress.

Company size

Fewer stress symptoms were reported by people in large companies than by those from smaller companies. Smaller companies seem to be more stressful. This relationship held true whether the company size was measured in terms of overall

Relocation attitude vs. ambition and job satisfaction

Willingness to relocate	Ambition score	Job satisfaction score
1. Happy to Move	35.2	29.9
2. Not Mind Moving	33.3	34.7
3. Prefer Not to Move	30.0	35.1

sales or the number of people in the individual's division.

Time in present job

As the length of time spent at the present job increased, stress symptoms decreased. Those in the first year of a new job reported stress symptoms significantly higher than in any other time period.

Number of companies worked for

Less stress was reported by those managers with experience in more than one company in the past 10 years than by those who had only worked in one company in that period.

Line or staff position

The results showed more symptoms of stress in line managers than in staff specialists, reflecting, perhaps, differences in responsibility and decision making capacities.

Smoking

Increasing stress symptoms were consistently associated with heavy smoking.

Exercise

Managers who attempted regularly to take exercise showed lower stress effects than those who did not.

Travelling

Stress was found to increase as the number of days per year of travelling increased.

We can state all of these findings another way. Suppose a hypothetical individual just starting his career in management were to plan a career strategy to minimize the risks of develop-

The mobile and the immobile manager

Willing to relocate	Unwilling to relocate
—under 45 years old	—over 45 years old
—single, or if married spouse is in favor of moving	—spouse is unwilling to move
—has a low or high educational level	—moderate educational level
—is in the higher pay brackets	—lower and middle income brackets
—has been in current location less than 5 years	—has been in current location more than 5 years
—has been at current job level less than 3 years	—has been at present job level more than 5 years
—does *not* feel satisfied with pay or organizational climate on reward	—*is* satisfied with pay and organizational climate on reward
—*high* level of ambition	—low level of ambition
—is *not* satisfied with his job	—*is* satisfied with his job
—is *not* worried about job security	—*is* worried about job security
—supervises hourly rated employees	—does *not* supervise hourly rated employees
—considers the organization as high on structure	—considers the organization low on structure
—does not consider organization warm and friendly	—considers the organization warm and friendly

ing stress symptoms. If guarding against stress were the main object of his career strategy, and if he were to follow the patterns suggested in this research, then he should first of all begin in senior management.

Given that this is an option open to very few indeed, he should at least try to start at the highest possible salary and be particularly sensitive about the first year in a new job. He should work for large, low-growth companies and preferably in a staff position. Once in a while he should move from company to company and he should also move between functional areas. Travelling and geographic moves should be minimized, and he should make a specific attempt to exercise and refrain from smoking.

Now, obviously, life might be pretty dull for our hypothetical

31

individual. In fact, this isn't the best attitude toward stress. The best attitude is not one of stress elimination but of containment and allocation.

In the natural process of growing, maturing and improving on our abilities some stress must be involved. In fact, there can be too little as well as too much stress in a manager's life.

For the individual, what's most important in life will also be the most stressful. The key issue in stress is the balance we strike between longing and striving. The goals we set and the energy we invest in their pursuit are the most important determinants of the stress we experience.

Rusting out or burning out?

If management stress is a problem in corporate life, then it has two forms the organization must address:

1. Those who are rusting out.
2. Those who are burning out.

The "rustouts" are those who have risen to a level (perhaps their level of incompetence) and have "settled-in." These managers are often stagnating and may in fact be obsolescent. Their obsolescence may be the result of being in a job that has become obsolescent, or the job may have changed to the degree that their skills and abilities are obsolescent. These managers often have little or nothing to do.

The opposite problem is that of the manager who is burning out. Here we encounter the image of the ambitious, aggressive and impatient individual who works 12 hours a day, travels continuously and drinks milk to soothe his executive ulcer.

Interestingly, both of these individuals are actually operating at extremes resulting in less than optimal managerial performance. The general relationship between job pressure and performance is that as job pressure increases, performance increases up to a certain point and declines thereafter. The managerial rustout lacks enough pressure in his job to secure his best performance. The managerial burnout has too much pressure, has passed the peak, and is on the downside of the performance curve. See the charts on pages 86-87.

What a manager has to do, obviously, is learn to live at the top part of the curve—not too much pressure, not too little. Managing subordinates involves the same issue. There shouldn't be too much stress, nor should there be too little, to secure the best performance.

The issue, of course, as most managers well know, isn't quite this simple. For, while almost all individuals follow performance curves of the same general shape, their curves are in different places. Individual A reaches his best performance at higher levels of job pressure than does individual B. Individual C, on the other hand, shows only small gains in performance for wide changes in job pressure.

What a manager must do, of course, is "know his men"—which ones would be more productive with more pressure and which ones with less. The productivity of managers depends on this relationship.

Job pressure and stress

Job pressure and stress are obviously related. The relationship, however, is very often misunderstood. The rustout and the burnout can very easily suffer from the same amount of stress. In fact, in most cases, the rustout is a far more serious problem both psychologically and in terms of physical health. The rustouts are also more tragic—often becoming depressed and even suicidal.

The protection the burnouts have is that they often enjoy their job. This job satisfaction has a great capacity to modify the effects of living at an accelerated pace. In our own research, we have found job satisfaction and stress symptoms to be inversely related. The more an individual is satisfied with his job and career, the fewer stress symptoms he reports.

In addition, from the results of a 15-year study it was found that the best predictor of longevity was job satisfaction. It was a better predictor than a whole range of variables often thought to be related to how long you're going to live.

In more general terms, our research on stress has impressed us by how much better it is for the individual to run too fast than too slow. Consequently, when making decisions that influence the pressure and tensions of the job, it would seem better to err on the side of too much rather than too little pressure.

In fact, understaffed organizations generally seem to have higher morale, a greater team spirit and a greater commitment to organization goals.

In one sense, the managerial rustout and the managerial burnout are only manifestations of a more fundamental problem faced by every organization and every manager. That problem involves the maintenance of managerial effectiveness. As noted earlier, becoming an effective manager is the first problem, and maintaining that effectiveness is the second. These and other issues will be explored in later chapters.

2. Your behavior and goals

About aggressiveness and ambition, disease and death

HE'S a familiar figure in many organizations: the aggressively competitive, restless, hard-driving and ambitious manager. Almost instinctively you know that he's headed for advancement to bigger and better jobs.

However, you—*and he*—probably don't realize that this kind of behavior may incur a heavy personal cost. And you may not be aware that ambition itself, though it can have benefits, also may extract a personal toll.

If you display the characteristics of the clock-racing corporate striver, you're almost surely a "Type A" individual. You're subject to constant bouts with stress, and there are high odds that you're on a collision course with heart disease.

Dr. Meyer Friedman and Dr. Ray Rosenman, who recently described the syndrome in their book *Type A Behavior and Your Heart*, found that this phenomenon is closely linked to coronary heart disease. Through research, they've been able to demonstrate that Type A behavior is a significant risk factor in heart disease *in its own right*, independent of the traditional risk factors such as high blood pressure, cigarette smoking, elevated blood fats and heredity.

Type A behavior

The Type A individual, as described by Friedman and Rosenman, is characterized by intense drive and aggressiveness. He's ambitious and competitive. He feels a constant pressure to get things done, and often pits himself against the clock.

He carries with him a constant sense of time urgency—a hurriedness in almost all aspects of his life. He's a restless person who has tremendous difficulty with idleness, generally equating idle time with wasted time.

The Type A person is a hard worker, very decisive, usually making decisions quickly. He speaks fast, directly to the point, and uses very few words. He's the type who's called a "polyphasic thinker," in that he likes to think about and do several things at the same time.

He moves, walks and eats rapidly, and feels impatient at the rate at which most events take place. He tends to schedule more and more in less and less time, often caught in a chronic and excessive struggle with one or a group of persons, either by preference or necessity.

You can test yourself for Type A characteristics by answering the questionnaire at the end of this chapter.

This behavior pattern doesn't seem to stem solely from the individual's personality, but often emerges when certain challenges or conditions arise, eliciting this particular response or complex of responses in what we call a "susceptible individual." In other words, we can describe Type A behavior as one outcome of an encounter between a "susceptible individual" and conditions in his job or career. The other outcome is a potential heart attack.

This is an important discovery, because nearly 50% of all premature deaths among males are from coronary disease. In fact, if you're a male over 40, you have about a 50/50 chance of dying from heart disease. In addition, only about 25% of all coronary disease can be explained on the basis of the traditional risk factors. That is, if blood pressure, cigarette smoking, cholesterol and heredity could be controlled, only about 25% of all heart disease would likely be eliminated. Therefore an astonishing 75% remains largely unexplained.

Some of this 75% is accounted for by diabetes and other factors, but a large part of the mystery remains to be solved. The fact that our day-to-day behavioral habits and behavioral style have been shown to be a significant and independent risk factor is an important contribution.

This is especially important for managers because, as research has clearly shown, of all employees they're particularly exposed to job and career elements that can produce Type A behavior.

In contrast to the Type A individual is the Type B. Rosenman and Friedman note that Type B individuals have significantly less risk of coronary heart disease, and are mainly free of such pronounced personality and behavioral traits. In short, they have no pressing conflict with either time or people, and so they're relatively free of any chronic sense of urgency or hostility.

The important aspect of the Type A behavior pattern is its relationship to coronary heart disease, which was clearly demonstrated in the eight-and-a-half-year study of 3,500 men done by Rosenman and Friedman.

The two researchers reported that Type A individuals had been more than twice as prone to the onset of clinical coronary disease, five times more prone to a second heart attack, and they've had fatal heart attacks twice as frequently.

Type A behavior and the organization

As a part of our own research study on management stress, the authors of this book have classified managerial subjects as Type A or Type B, and noted some of the patterns in organization life.

While the polar opposites of this syndrome are defined as Type A and Type B, there are actually four behavioral categories: A_1, A_2, B_3 and B_4. The A_1 and B_4 categories represent fully developed or extreme Type A and Type B behavior. A_2 and B_3 represent Type A and Type B behavior in a less-developed form.

We can classify individuals into one of these four types at the end of a 30-minute interview, in which general appearance and certain characteristic motor activities (brisk and impatient body movements, fist-clenching in ordinary conversation, taut facial musculature, explosive and hurried speech patterns, upper chest breathing, and lack of body relaxation) make the detection of the behavior pattern relatively easy.

In addition to these visually perceived characteristics, we ask the subject a series of about 25 carefully structured questions dealing with the degree and intensity of his (1) ambition, (2) drive, (3) competitive, aggressive and hostile feelings, and (4) sense of time urgency.

It's important to emphasize that, in assessing the behavior pattern from the interview, we usually consider the individual's manner or style of responding more important than the content of his answers.

Of the managers in our stress study, approximately 60% were classified as Type A's. And 27% were classified as the extreme Type A_1. Only 12% of the respondents were the fully developed Type B_4.

These percentages are similar to those reported by Rosenman, who observed that in the period 1960-1961 nearly half of his 3,500 male subjects exhibited Type A behavior. Rosenman has speculated that the frequency of Type A behavior has increased significantly since then, and now might run as high as 75% due to greatly increased socioeconomic pressures. Rosenman believes that Type A behavior has been increasing in industrialized societies in general.

Our findings support these observations. We've found that, in some companies, the incidence of Type A behavior runs as high as 76%. We've also found a higher incidence of Type A behavior in high-growth companies.

It's interesting to speculate whether the company growth might have caused the Type A behavior, or whether the Type A behavior caused the company growth.

We examined age and education with regard to their influence on Type A behavior. There were no significant trends in terms of education level, although we saw a slight indication that lower levels of education were associated with a greater prevalence of Type A behavior. Type A behavior declined slightly with age, while Type B behavior increased slightly.

It was amply clear that the highest percentage of Type A_1

behavior occurred in the age group 36 to 55—peak years in which many issues of job and career take on a sense of urgency.

Type A behavior and health

In our research, we used several measures of health in examining differences between the Type A and Type B managers. These included a stress-symptom checklist (like the one examined in chapter one), blood tests, exercise tests and a survey of health habits. We found that the Type A's and particularly the A_1's, stand out as significantly different on a number of factors.

All Type A's showed higher blood pressure, both systolic and diastolic, in comparison to the Type B's. The Type A_1's recorded the highest levels of blood pressure and blood content of cholesterol and triglycerides. (Triglycerides are a blood fat somewhat similar to cholesterol.)

In addition to these factors, we found that a larger percentage of the Type A_1's may have lower cardiovascular or aerobic fitness. In short, we found Type A_1's to be particularly high on a number of coronary risk factors.

In fact, it can be predicted that Type A_1 managers incur about a 50% greater risk of coronary heart disease, based on traditional risk factors alone.

Type A behavior and work habits

All of the participants in our study hold managerial positions, and we asked a number of questions about their work habits. We found that the Type A_1's put in the longest work week, work more discretionary hours per week, and travel more days per year.

In addition, the A_1's are slightly less satisfied with their jobs.

We also examined job conditions associated with Type A's, and found the following to be the most responsible for eliciting Type A behavior:

1. Having supervisory responsibility for people.
2. Feeling that you're working in competition with others.
3. Excessive workloads.

4. Conflicting demands in the job.

In addition to these job conditions, two other factors served to differentiate the Type A manager.

First, we found that Type A managers make more money than do Type B individuals. A greater percentage of the Type A managers earned above the median salary.

Second, we found that Type A managers have a strong sense of personal confidence. For example, they feel it's relatively easy for them to move between organizations if they so desire, and that their skills and abilities are adequate both for their present and future jobs.

The pathways of stress

Our studies have enabled us to visualize, we think, one of the central pathways of management stress:

1. High-growth companies, in particular, tend to produce the managerial job conditions listed above: supervisory responsibility; competitiveness; heavy workloads; conflicting demands.
2. Mix these conditions with "susceptible individuals" — influenced to some extent by educational background and age.
3. Those individuals exhibit Type A behavior, which appears to produce higher levels of coronary risk.
4. The Type A's also seem to experience more stress symptoms and greater feelings of job dissatisfaction.
5. But Type A behavior also seems to have its rewards, in that managers of this type appear to be more successful (in salary, at any rate).

The illustration opposite shows in graphic form how we view this pathway of stress.

We must point out that high corporate growth is thought to be only one of a number of factors responsible for producing the job conditions that tend to elicit Type A behavior. Other factors of equal or possibly more importance may include company size, structure, climate, and leadership style.

The pathways of managerial stress

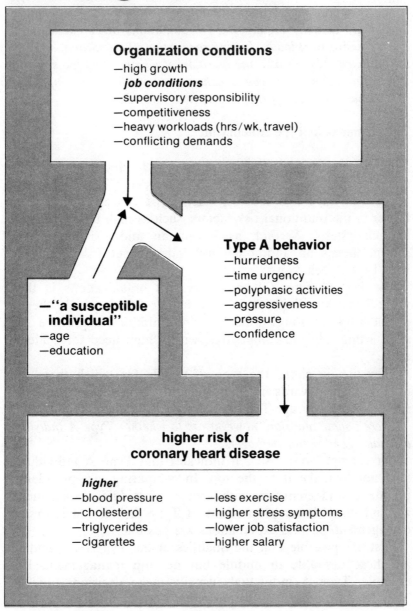

Organization conditions
—high growth
job conditions
—supervisory responsibility
—competitiveness
—heavy workloads (hrs/wk, travel)
—conflicting demands

Type A behavior
—hurriedness
—time urgency
—polyphasic activities
—aggressiveness
—pressure
—confidence

—"a susceptible
individual"
—age
—education

**higher risk of
coronary heart disease**

higher
—blood pressure
—cholesterol
—triglycerides
—cigarettes

—less exercise
—higher stress symptoms
—lower job satisfaction
—higher salary

Furthermore, we're not yet absolutely sure of what's cause and what's effect. The five points above are only an interpretation of what we believe to be the sequence of events. In some instances, there's still considerable doubt about the relationships.

For instance, there's the question of whether the "susceptible individual" actually creates the job conditions of competitiveness and excessive workloads. In this sense, the job conditions may be self-inflicted. There's also the question of whether low job satisfaction is an outcome of Type A behavior or whether it's simply one of the characteristics of the "susceptible individuals."

The dilemmas in Type A behavior

About one thing, however, there's little doubt: the higher coronary risk associated with Type A behavior. This higher risk appears to have two sources. First, Type A's appear to score higher in the traditional risk factors, such as high blood pressure and cholesterol. Second, as Rosenman and Friedman have shown, there's an additional and independent risk associated with Type A behavior.

The big dilemma for managers and organizations is that, while Type A individuals incur a higher coronary risk, they're people who get things done. They're ambitious, aggressive and self-starting. They're competitive, with a high need for achievement.

They are, in short, the type of people for which there are usually high rewards in management. Organizations usually reward and encourage Type A behavior.

There's some question, however, as to whether Type A individuals make good senior managers.

For example, our research indicates that Type A individuals tend not to make it to the top. In comparing vice-presidents, presidents and chairmen with groups of middle management, we find much lower proportions of Type A individuals in top management. Several explanations are possible.

First, it's possible that the qualities of the Type A individual are those desirable in middle but not top management. For example, Type A individuals usually make decisions quickly. They have little capacity to postpone. Usually, they're too busy doing the thing right, to do the right thing. At the top, wisdom in decision making is valued more than speed. In addition, Type A individuals are often *too* competitive. They make other people nervous. These appear to be qualities not valued in selecting people for top-management jobs.

A second explanation, of course, is that managers change. While in middle management, Type A behavior may be functional for getting ahead. As one progresses and becomes older, there may, in fact, be a mellowing—a "settling-in" effect where the individual starts to come to grips with his ambition and mobility aspirations. This mellowing may result in a change away from Type A behavior.

A third explanation is that Type A managers may simply die off earlier, diminishing the numbers available for promotion to the top. We might call this a sorting out, or a kind of natural selection.

Fourth, we might say that the conditions of the job at the top are such that they tend not to elicit Type A behavior. Consequently, both the mellowing that comes with age and the conditions in the job may combine to negate the prevalence of Type A behavior.

Each of these explanations has some value, and they all probably combine to account for the fewer Type A individuals in top management.

Type A and creativity

Our experience also has led us to speculate on other aspects of the Type A personality. For example, we believe that Type A traits may stunt the individual's creative potential.

It's well known that new creative insights are most likely to occur in a certain setting. The individual first intensely ponders a problem, then leaves it, passing a few hours or perhaps a few days in minor illness, fishing or reading—usually an activity with a large component of solitude. Somewhere near the end of that interval, often as he's about to re-enter the arena, a fresh and effective approach to the problem strikes him and he returns to work with great excitement.

It's this potentially fertile interval that the Type A finds threat-

ening and avoids—but at great cost to his potential.

Try to imagine a Type A personality in an art gallery. He would likely try to see, and perhaps categorize, as many paintings as time permitted. We can't envisage a Type A personality studying a painting for half an hour, or going back to look at the same painting again and again.

Thus, we suspect that many windows of perception are closed to him. Type A individuals frequently don't permit themselves to discover the meaning that would transform an experience into a heightened form.

If this is true, it's a great tragedy—a consequence that the individual would little have suspected when he embarked on the road of excessive competitiveness, an ever-increasing workload and the insidious, largely self-imposed recurring deadlines.

The early description of the Type A syndrome, "the Sisyphus complex," was apt. Indeed, the Type A individual may largely spend his time pushing that huge boulder to the top of the hill, with no genuine respite when he gets there—simply the return to the valley as quickly as possible to begin all over again.

Coping with Type A behavior

Despite all the risks and drawbacks, we must emphasize again that Type A behavior isn't all bad.

Type A individuals are very productive people. Their problem is that they tend to be *over*-competitive and *over*-driven. They seem to be constantly doing more and more in less and less time. They're continuously running—motivated in a suicidal way. They're not only burning the candle at both ends, but they've divided it and have it burning at several.

Since it's difficult to modify this behavior, short of a heart attack, and even then not always, prevention takes on greater importance. Type A individuals, especially those over 40, should regularly monitor and control the traditional major risk factors in heart disease: blood pressure, smoking and blood fats. They should also try to modify their behavior by both slowing down internally and doing some re-engineering of their lives.

More than others under stress, the Type A individual needs to stop running and start living—operating by the calendar and not the stopwatch. Perhaps this way he can be productive and live to enjoy it.

Ambition and stress

As you've just seen, one of the characteristics of a Type A individual is almost obsessive ambition—a relentless *longing* to rise in the organization. However, it's important to realize that, while all Type A people are ambitious, all ambitious people are not Type A.

Ambition is a strong desire or need. On the other hand, Type A behavior is a way of acting.

In dealing with ambition, we must point out again that no issue is more fundamental to stress than the balance we strike between longing and striving.

The goals we set for ourselves and the energy we spend in pursuing them are key determinants of our physical and psychological health. Our goals, while challenging, must be balanced and realistic. And the energy invested in the pursuit of ambitions must be matched to our capacity.

It may be that some managers have begun to understand this relationship subtly, if not consciously. In chapter one, for example, we examined trends among managers to put up a growing resistance to geographic relocation, which generally implies promotion. Managers may be developing a sensitivity to the fact that making a life is as important as making a living.

For ambitious managers, no matter what their behavior pattern, there will always be the problem of disappointment. Unfulfilled ambition is universal. It only varies in intensity.

Managers clearly recognize the problems of disappointment, though they seldom articulate it. The reality of pyramid-shaped organizations is hard to deny. While all may strive, not all will achieve. With the passage of time, high ambition must be cooled; the disappointment must be managed.

At its best, the process involves a re-evaluation of goals, capacities and opportunities—a closer matching with reality. At its worst, it involves protest, despair and withdrawal.

Consequently, there's always a risk in high ambition, and that risk is failure and disappointment. As a result, the strength to manage disappointment can be fundamental to the strength of desire to rise in the organization and the consequent willingness to assume leadership.

Clearly, then, the fear of failing in one's career can be the roadblock to success.

Managers have worried over fulfilling their ambitions since the birth of organized society. But the new generation of managers may be particularly susceptible to these concerns. They belong to a culture where parents and educators have served their young proteges by doing their utmost to smooth every obstacle and minimize every source of suffering and distress.

There have been benefits from such behavior, but there have also been costs. If the individual has been uniquely successful in avoiding pain, he also has become uniquely vulnerable to the fear of encountering frustration and disappointment in the future.

Unfortunately, the implication isn't trivial. Only those who come to terms with the fear of failure can escape a nervous preoccupation with the future. Those who don't will continue to experience anxiety that can be appeased only momentarily by fresh achievements.

It's important to understand that the anxiety will be chronic, because the attainment of a goal leads quickly to a new challenge even more difficult than the last.

However, we mustn't measure the implication merely in anxiety. The individual can learn to live with that, although it will rob him of many satisfactions. The real price lies in the pervasive unwillingness to run the risk of failure—even to achieve objectives that must be reached to lead a full and productive life.

There are risks on both sides. High ambition risks the disappointment of failure; low ambition, the lost opportunity to discover one's own capabilities and achieve a full life.

For the manager, high ambition means preparing to take the maximum responsibility. It means making it to the top—the willingness to assume leadership. Yet, as we've seen, there appears a growing disillusionment as to whether the objective is worth achieving.

The problems up top are tough, the responsibilities heavy.

And there's the constant innuendo that success, while obviously the result of ability and hard work, somehow comes at the expense of others. Another source of disillusionment implies that, while the goal itself is worthwhile, the costs along the way may be too high.

Ambition, in fact, has come under attack.

There's ample evidence to support the point that ambition has largely gone out of style. A recent American Management Association survey noted that managers used to define success by career advancement, material reward and recognition. But the new criteria included job satisfaction, meaningful work, domestic tranquility and good health. The old criteria were closely associated with ambition. The new criteria lack this emphasis, and indicate a reappraisal of values.

Such changes also have important implications in terms of motivation. A man satisfied with his job, who considers his work meaningful, and who's in good health with a happy family, will weigh very carefully the opportunity for more responsibility when the major benefits are things he may no longer prize.

A manager with such attitudes is, of course, somewhat of an enigma to the corporation. A manager who turns down promotion disrupts the traditional mobility pattern. This raises questions about the man's ambition, and those responsible for the career and job-rotation system face still more complex problems.

A recent survey conducted among corporations in the United States showed that one out of three managers was turning down promotion. The research pointed out that these changing attitudes were reducing the reservoir of managerial talent available to growing, geographically diversified companies.

The study also pointed out that, while in the past the manager reluctant to rise in the organization could be merely shelved and forgotten, the no-promotion attitude is now so common that such procedures would irreparably damage a company.

Companies must rethink their policies: What should they do now when a manager turns down a promotion? How should they handle those who choose to "bow out"?

Part of the disenchantment with ambition has to do with an evaluation of its costs. Making it to the top is associated with long hours, hard work and high stress. Domestic tranquility may also be a problem.

But are the consequences of ambition all bad? Aren't our major achievements associated with high ambition and willingness to risk failure? What really are the patterns associated with the ambitious manager?

Ambition and the modern manager

As a part of our research in the area of management stress, the authors have developed an instrument to measure how ambitious an individual is to move up in the organization.* Over the years we've gathered considerable data, which include personality variables, job and career variables, and a number of indicators of health and fitness.

Since ambition is fundamental to stress, we examined the relationships that appear to differentiate the more ambitious from the less ambitious manager. Profiles of the two types appear opposite.

We found a small but significant correlation between ambition and age. As the individual grows older, he becomes less ambitious. The older individual may have achieved many of his goals or cooled-out his ambition, coming to grips with the probability of future achievement. He may also have changed his desire for promotion after re-assessing the activities in life he values.

The lessening of ambition with age seems to be a natural consequence of both the stages in the life cycle and the reality of pyramid structures.

We also found a correlation between ambition and education. Those managers with some university education were generally more ambitious than those without. We can account for part of this by the fact that more of the younger managers tend to be university educated. The effect of education, however, is proba-

* By ambition we mean the strength of the desire to rise in the organization.

Ambition and managerial characteristics

Less ambitious	More ambitious
Older	*Younger*
No university education	Some university education

—Personality—

Less ambitious	More ambitious
—affected by feeling	—emotionally stable, calm
—shy, restrained	—venturesome, socially bold
—apprehensive, worrying	—confident, self-assured
—reserved, aloof	—outgoing, participating
—low need for achievement	—high need for achievement
—sees change as negative	—sees change as positive

—Work—

Less ambitious	More ambitious
—shorter hours, less travel	—more hours, more travel
—satisfaction with supervision and pay	—dissatisfaction with supervision and pay
—less work satisfaction	—more work satisfaction
—locked in, stagnating	—not locked in, not stagnating
—plays it safe	—enjoys a calculated risk
—less time with superiors	—more time with superiors

—Career—

Less ambitious	More ambitious
—more successful than hoped	—less successful than hoped
—less willing to move	—more willing to move
—more satisfied	—less satisfied

—Health—

Less ambitious	More ambitious
—more symptoms and days off work	—fewer symptoms and days off work
—affected by stress and tension of job	—not affected by stress and tension of job
—more cigarettes, less exercise	—less cigarettes, more exercise

Less ambitious	More ambitious
Type B	*Type A*
—lower coronary risk	—higher coronary risk

bly complex, linked to both the early personality development of the individual and the process of a university education itself.

Ambition and personality

As noted earlier, we define ambition as the strength of desire to move up in the organization. And in the folklore of management, we often portray ambitious individuals as being ruthless, slightly neurotic and without scruples. But in the authors' assessment of the personality of the ambitious manager, we've found a pattern that fails to support this stereotype.

Our data show that ambitious managers are calm, mature and emotionally stable. They adjust to new demands easily, and have a number of characteristics often associated with organization leaders. They're confident and self-assured about their own abilities. Socially, they tend to be venturesome and spontaneous, often thought of as easy-going and warm-hearted. They generally get along well, and have the capacity to face the wear and tear of dealing with people and gruelling emotional situations.

The ambitious manager also scores high on the need for achievement. He aspires to accomplish difficult tasks, maintains high standards, and is willing to work hard toward distant goals. He responds positively to competition, and is willing to put forth effort to attain excellence.

The ambitious manager also rates high in his capacity to deal with change. He likes new and different experiences, dislikes routine and avoids it. He can change his opinions and values in different circumstances, and adapts readily to his environment.

Overall, the ambitious manager would be considered well adjusted with a number of leadership capabilities. Psychologically, he's in good health and well prepared for the job and career of management.

Ambition and work patterns

As you might expect, the ambitious manager works longer days, more discretionary hours per week, and he travels more days per year than the less ambitious manager. In this sense, he works harder.

50

Overall, his level of job satisfaction isn't much different than the less ambitious manager's, although he tends to be more satisfied with his work and promotion and less satisfied with his supervision and pay. He apparently likes what he's doing, but is discontent with the recognition he receives.

He doesn't feel he's stagnating nor does he feel locked into his present organization. In most cases, he reports his job as exhilarating rather than fatiguing. The riskiness and challenge in his job are the elements he responds to most favorably. He enjoys taking a calculated risk, and abhors a strategy of playing it safe.

You can also characterize ambitious managers by how they allocate their time between superiors, peers and subordinates. Those high on ambition spend considerably more time with superiors and less with peers and subordinates. Perhaps this reflects a stronger identification with the problems of their superiors and less with those of peers. It may also reflect a desire for visibility and a conscious effort to promote their own careers.

Ambition and career

On the issue of career, the ambitious manager is more dissatisfied than his less ambitious counterpart. He reports that with regard to his career, at this particular stage, he's less successful than he'd hoped to be.

Within his own organization, he's more willing to move geographically—movement usually being associated with career advancement. He's also much more willing to change organizations, even without an increase in rewards and responsibilities. He responds favorably to challenge, and almost never finds that more is expected of him than he can deliver.

Ambition, stress and health

Generally speaking, the ambitious manager appears to be in better health than his less ambitious counterpart. He reports fewer stress symptoms and significantly fewer days off work because of illness. In addition, he doesn't consider that his work affects his health adversely, and, in most cases, he sees himself under less stress and tension than other managers with the same responsibility. He also seems less affected by common job frustrations such as constant telephone interruptions, scheduled meetings and the inability to concentrate on a single problem for very long.

In terms of health habits, the ambitious manager is more likely to be a non-smoker. In addition, if he does smoke, he reports fewer cigarettes per day. He also reports getting more exercise off the job, although his fitness level isn't much different from the less ambitious manager's.

Given all this, one might conclude that it's better to be more ambitious rather than less ambitious.

There are, however, two variables on which the ambitious manager is at greater risk. He runs a greater risk of developing coronary heart disease from traditional causes, and he's also more likely to exhibit Type A behavior.

Ambition and Type A behavior

As described earlier in this chapter, one of the characteristics of the Type A manager is his ambition. And, flipping the coin over, our studies show that the ambitious are much more likely to be Type A. And Type A's, as you've seen, have an independent coronary risk all their own.

Our research also examined the coronary risk of managers in the traditional way. We measured their values on known risk factors in heart disease (blood pressure, cholesterol, diabetes and heredity), and found again that the more ambitious have a higher incidence of these traditional risk factors.

It seems amply clear from *both* the Type A syndrome *and* the traditional heart-disease risk factors that one of the costs of great ambition is very high coronary risk.

The hazards, then, of great ambition are (1) failure, (2) disappointment and (3) heart disease.

For the ambitious, the best possible hedge against heart disease would seem to be modifying Type A behavior and keeping the traditional risk factors at normal levels.

There's no easy hedge against the possibility of failure and disappointment. Those, however, who have other avenues of life in which to channel the emotions and energy of disappointment would seem well prepared.

In other words, the especially ambitious would be better off not to load all their eggs in one basket. Don't aim all your longing in one direction.

Those with heavy commitments and strong psychological investments in a particular career or endeavor and who, consequently, run a high risk of failure or disappointment, need other substantive interests or activities to fall back on. This is especially true of those individuals who make work and career the singular, overriding activity of their lives.

Making a life means choosing how we invest our time and activity. For most individuals, there are four general areas— which might be called the "four baskets of life." They are: (1) Work, (2) Family, (3) Self and (4) Community. Into each of these areas we proportion our time and activity, and at different stages of life the proportions are more or less appropriate. People sometimes make these choices consciously, sometimes by the gradual accumulation of a number of small decisions. You can think of your own strategy for living in terms of how you distribute "the eggs of life" among these four baskets.

From this analogy, a few simple observations would seem self-evident:

1. How you apportion your time and activity among the four baskets is more or less appropriate at different stages of life.
2. A strategy of investing all your time and activity in one or two baskets is a high-risk strategy in terms of disappointment.
3. Shifting your investments of time and activity between baskets rather quickly demands heavy psychological work— especially if you've almost entirely neglected one area for a long period of time.
4. For some investments, the opportunity occurs only once. If lost, it becomes difficult or impossible to regain.
5. There is probably a quality as well as a quantity aspect to the investment of time and activity in each of the areas.

The analogy, of course, can't be pushed too far. Understanding how and why people make their choices for living is difficult and complex—related to values, personality, opportunity and other factors.

Perhaps, however, the analogy does help to explain a common phenomenon: the rather severe changes experienced by many individuals at the time of retirement. These types of people have often been ambitious, with heavy psychological investments in work and career. What they have often failed to do in life is to invest in the basket called Self. By Self we mean those activities that you might do, not for your family, not for your work and not for your community, but only because you personally enjoy the activity. Activities such as painting, writing, sports, music and hobbies come to mind at once.

If, during one's active working life, no substantial investments have been made in activities for the Self, retirement can be tragic.

At retirement, the individual has the psychological problem of shifting eggs between baskets. He no longer has Work in which to invest time and activity, and Family is reduced, with usually only the spouse left for active involvement. There are some Community activities available—but usually limited in scope. The individual must turn in large part to Self. The turn can be tragic if, during the 40 years of active working life, no previous investments have been made in the area. Substitution for the psychological loss associated with retirement from work becomes difficult in the extreme. The problem of retirement has its origins in an earlier stage of life where the individual has failed to invest in Self.

The highly ambitious have, consequently, two good reasons for maintaining substantive interests outside of their career: (1) the problem of managing disappointment in the face of failure, and (2) the problem of retirement.

Disappointment, of course, must be squarely faced. By avoiding it, the individual robs himself of a full and productive life. It seems clear that those of us lucky enough to have learned from childhood how to face loss are best equipped to deal with the personal issues that arise during experiences of disappointment.

As in all matters of personal development, however, the outcome turns on the quality of the person, the measure of the courage he can mobilize, the richness of his talents and his ability to understand himself.

Testing your own behavior

Are you a Type A individual or a Type B? To obtain an estimate of your behavior type, answer the following questions by indicating the response that *most often* applies to you.

	Yes	No
1. Were you on any athletic or other teams or activities in high school or college?	_____	_____
2. Did you strive to be a leader on these teams?	_____	_____
3. Since you began making your living, did you or do you now go to night school or other schools to improve your chances for advancement?	_____	_____
4. Are you satisfied with your present job?	_____	_____
5. When younger, did you consciously strive for advancement?	_____	_____
6. Do you still strive for advancement?	_____	_____

Typically, the Type A individual will be found to have (1) played on athletic teams, (2) gone to night or further school, (3) felt dissatisfaction with his present position, and (4) participated in various organizations.

7. Do you think of yourself as hard-
driving and aggressive?   _____   _____

8. Does your wife think of you as
hard-driving and aggressive?   _____   _____

9. Do you strive for the admiration
and respect of your friends and
working associates—in contrast to their
affection?   _____   _____

10. When you play games with your
children (or the children of others) do
you purposely let them win?   _____   _____

11. When you play games with friends,
do you give it all you're worth?   _____   _____

12. Do you play mainly to win—in
contrast to having fun?   _____   _____

13. Is there much competition in your
work?   _____   _____

14. Do you enjoy the competition in
your work?   _____   _____

15. Do you usually drive your car just
beyond the speed limit?   _____   _____

16. Does it irritate you to be held up
by a slower car in front of you?   _____   _____

The Type A individual may not think of himself as hard-
driving and aggressive, but invariably he'll admit that his wife
believes he is. He typically prefers respect and admiration to

affection, and rarely allows his children to win at any game. He always plays to win and enjoys the competition. He becomes excessively irritated at slower drivers and, although often angry, goes out of his way to conceal such feelings.

	Yes	No
17. Are there many deadlines in your work and do you find them exciting?	_____	_____
18. Do you find you get more done working against deadlines?	_____	_____
19. When you have an appointment with someone, will you usually be there on time?	_____	_____
20. Does it bother you to be kept waiting?	_____	_____
21. Do you spend time on hobbies only when there's nothing more important to do?	_____	_____
22. Do you get impatient when you see something being done at work slower than you think it should be done?	_____	_____
23. Do you often try to get something else done when eating alone?	_____	_____
24. Do you usually eat quickly and get on to other things?	_____	_____
25. Do you plan your activities so you don't have to wait?	_____	_____

26. When someone else is talking, do

you ever try to hurry them along? _____ _____

27. Do you feel you have the time to
get everything done you want to? _____ _____

The Type A individual usually believes that he has deadlines, but he enjoys them. He's invariably punctual and it annoys him greatly to be kept waiting by others. He rarely has time for hobbies, and when he does they're as competitive as his vocation. He dislikes helping in routine jobs and will do a job himself because he grows impatient watching others who may be slower. The Type A often does more than one thing at a time; he walks fast, and rarely remains long at the dinner table. He invariably dislikes waiting for anything, will rush others along and constantly feels that time is passing too quickly.

Type A behavior can be determined accurately only by a structured interview—which could include these typical questions. However, if you've answered "yes" to most of these questions, you're more than likely a Type A person. The structured interview technique was developed by the Western Collaborative Study Group.*

The next chapter will deal with coronary heart disease—its links with stress, Type A behavior and the traditional risk factors.

* The Western Collaborative Study Group: Ray H. Rosenman, M.D.; Meyer Friedman, M.D.; Reuben Straus, M.D.; Moses Wurm, M.D.; Robert Kositchek, M.D.; Wilfrid Hahn, Ph.D.; Nicholas T. Werthessen, Ph.D.

3. Coronary heart disease

About risks and behavior,
rehabilitation and survival

JOHN S. SLOAN was entitled to feel pleased with himself. A professional engineer, at age 41, he possessed all the contemporary hallmarks of success: a happy marriage, two teenage boys who were doing well at school, a comfortable house (almost paid for) in a desirable neighborhood, and the imminent prospect of promotion to company vice-president.

Mind you, he hadn't had too much time of late to count his blessings. A year previously the company plant started moving to a new location and, as production manager, he had found himself involved in a hectic work schedule. Even Mary, his usually so-patient wife, began to express concern as six- and seven-day work weeks became routine. Still, the job had to be done and "goodness only knows what a mess things would get into if I wasn't there to keep tabs on everything."

Besides, when the move was completed, he could ease off a bit, maybe "play a little golf, or take a week's vacation and get in a little fishing." Maybe he would cut back on his smoking too; with all his stress and strain, he was up to a pack and a half a day now ... wouldn't do any harm to lose a little weight also, but that was difficult when one's meals consisted of an endless succession of hurried sandwiches interspersed with "two-martini luncheon meetings" and expense-account dinners.

Yes, he probably was a little out of shape . . . which no doubt accounted for the heartburn and indigestion pain he had begun to experience in recent months whenever he got up-tight at work or tried to lift anything heavy. He was "probably developing a peptic ulcer," the almost prestigious occupational disease of all successful executives.

In due course, John's plant completed its move to the new location. But the transition phase brought with it teething problems which, naturally, only John could solve. Admittedly, weekends at the office were no longer routine (although they did occur from time to time), but the 12- and 13-hour workday became commonplace.

Always a hard driver, he was now hotly in pursuit of the presidency, and he dedicated himself to the task with all the energy and determination which had characterized his performance as one of the best linemen of his university football team. Unfortunately, he wasn't in his early twenties any more, and while he still possessed the spirit and motivation of bygone years, his body was no longer fit enough to endure the tasks he placed upon it.

His "indigestion" pain was bothering him more frequently now, and not only after eating. From time to time, he experienced severe discomfort in his upper abdomen and chest when he ran up a flight of stairs, or walked quickly up an incline (not that he did too much walking nowadays). Usually, the pain would go away if he belched or rested for a minute or so.

He began to feel chronically tired. Never at any time, however, did he feel that he had any serious health problem. After all, he had always come through the annual company medical examination with flying colors; blood pressure, electrocardiogram, blood and urine checks always normal . . . which was, after all, only to be expected in a strong, 6'2" ex-college football player.

Then one day, while sitting dozing in front of the television set, he got a fright; the stomach pain came on quite suddenly. Only on this occasion it was more severe and seemed to have moved up into his chest. For a moment or two, he had difficulty breathing, as the pain radiated first into his neck and jaw, and then down both arms to his hands. He found he was sweating profusely. He didn't know what to do. When he tried to lie down, the pain seemed to get worse; moving around didn't do any good, and neither did belching gas.

Mary, noticing his agitation and pale, sweating features, learned for the first time of his recurrent bouts of "indigestion." She wanted to call a doctor, but John persuaded her to wait and see if his condition improved. Fortunately (or unfortunately as it turned out), the pain subsided after about 30 minutes, although for the next day or two his chest felt very sore.

In deference to Mary's wishes, he called in to see his family physician the following week and told him that he had been getting the "occasional niggling stomach pain when I am over-tired or tense." A combination of John's natural tendency to downplay any evidence of physical weakness, together with what may have been a too-easy acceptance of his tale by the physician, led to a diagnosis of "nerves." An electrocardiogram was not carried out. Still, as John himself says, "hindsight is always 20/20."

During the following weeks, John continued his heavy work schedule, suffering only occasional and relatively mild "nerve" pains in his chest ... until the week the plant workers went on strike. If the job was hectic before, it was frenetic now. Extra duties, extra hours, unpleasantness on the picket lines, all contributed to bring about a desperate situation. There seemed to be no solution. As a matter of fact, there was, and in John's case, it was almost the final one.

At four o'clock one morning, he was awakened by the most severe pain in his chest he had ever experienced. It was as if a terrible weight was pressing on his chest bone, squeezing and squeezing until he felt he could no longer breathe. He thought he was going to die. He put up no argument when Mary called the ambulance and, within half an hour, an electrocardiogram was carried out in the emergency department and the young, serious-looking doctor quietly gave him the news: he had sustained a severe heart attack and was to be admitted to the coronary care unit immediately.

John was three weeks in hospital, during which time he

experienced a series of emotional reactions to his predicament. At first, he was stunned by the doctor's diagnosis. It was impossible for him to have had a heart attack; his heart wasn't weak; he had never had a day's illness in his life... there must be some mistake. This period of "denial" lasted about 48 hours. Some patients never lose it even after discharge from hospital, persisting in their belief that the doctors have "made a mistake." In John's case, it was replaced by a sullen anger. What right had fate to treat him in this unfair fashion? Hadn't he worked hard to make his mark in life, to provide for his wife and family, to get on? What reward was this for living according to the rules?

After he came out of intensive care, his cardiologist told him he would probably be able to go home "in a week or 10 days." Always a stickler for accuracy, John interpreted "a week" as being exactly seven days. When this period was up, he was told he might be in hospital for another "week." He now became dreadfully depressed. He felt the doctors were keeping something from him; he was going to die, or at best be an invalid for the rest of his life. He would never see his children again.

At the end of three weeks, he went home still in a depressed mood. The first day back in familiar surroundings was almost too much for him. He felt so fatigued he had to go to bed after only a few hours. He had lost his old aggressive self-confidence and was fearful of responsibility. Even after his return to work, ostensibly fully recovered, Mary was at first surprised and then perturbed to find that he continued to lean on her, reluctant to take the initiative in financial or domestic matters requiring a decision.

This state of affairs continued for some time. A lot of uncertainty remained in John Sloan's life. Would he be able to return to work? Should he return to the same job? How physically active would he be able to be? What should he do to help prevent a second heart attack? What really caused the first?*

* "The Case of John Sloan": reproduced with the permission of the publisher from *Heart Attack? Counterattack!* by Terence Kavanagh, M.D., copyright © 1976 Van Nostrand Reinhold Ltd., Toronto.

Risk factors

In some ways, our understanding of coronary heart disease today resembles our understanding of tuberculosis a century ago. One hundred years ago, the tubercle bacillus had just been discovered, but its causal connection with the common and devastating disease, tuberculosis, had not been realized.

Physicians had learned, however, from long clinical experience, that tuberculosis was more commonly seen in certain settings; it seemed particularly likely to occur in crowded living conditions in a damp climate and was seen most often in females in the first half of life.

Thus, physicians had noted several "risk factors" for tuberculosis. And, indeed, over the next 70 years, the main therapeutic aim of physicians in treating tuberculosis was to try to modify these risk factors. Sanatoria were built away from urban congestion. Patients were exposed to an abundance of fresh air, encouraged to eat a nutritious diet, to gain weight, to rest and avoid fatigue.

We now have identified several heart attack risk factors in a somewhat more scientific way. Individuals living in certain communities have been examined regularly and followed over many years. The best-known study of this type is the one carried out at Framingham, Mass. over a 20-year period. As time passed, a certain number of individuals developed various cardiovascular diseases, including coronary heart disease. The characteristics that were most closely correlated with the development of angina pectoris or a heart attack were identified and are now familiarly known as coronary risk factors.

In the Framingham study, the risk factors with the strongest correlation were an elevated level of cholesterol in the blood, cigarette smoking, high blood pressure, the presence of diabetes and evidence suggesting cardiac enlargement on the resting electrocardiogram.

Other studies have suggested that lack of exercise and certain behavior patterns may also be coronary risk factors. For example, Dr. Ralph Paffenbarger of San Francisco has shown that longshoremen doing heavy work have fewer heart attacks than those engaged in light duties. Dr. J. N. Morris in England has

Type A behavior and the arteries

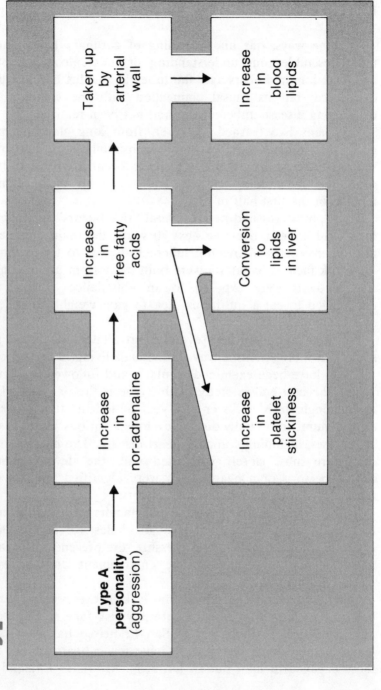

found that civil servants who engaged in vigorous exercise, such as jogging, in their leisure time have fewer heart attacks than those whose leisure habits involved either mild exercise or no exercise at all.

Finally, as described earlier, the Type A personality pattern is associated with an increased risk of developing clinically apparent coronary heart disease.

Thus, the available evidence has led to the construction of a coronary risk profile, with predicted susceptibility to coronary heart disease correlating with the number of existing risk factors.

Does modification of coronary risk factors reduce the chances of a heart attack? Theoretically, it would seem quite likely, but there are obviously other factors that play a part because every physician sees patients who have few or even no risk factors and who develop premature coronary heart disease.

The arterial wall

Although we do know a great deal about the process of thickening on the inner surface of the arterial wall, the exact mechanism isn't yet known, nor do we really understand the role the risk factors play. There's an interaction between platelets (small particles that circulate in the blood) when they stick to the side of the arterial wall and the cells in the lining of the wall itself. The result of the interaction is the deposition or formation of a lipid or fatty material in the wall, which gradually becomes larger and begins to narrow the blood passageway of the artery.

What, however, is the relationship with stress? A simple, hypothetical conception of how stress might operate to cause arterial thickening is shown in the schematic illustration on the opposite page.

Aggression is known to be accompanied by a rise in noradrenaline, a hormone produced in the adrenal gland. This hormone does many things necessary for health. But it also produces a rise in the amount of fatty acids in the blood, and these in turn increase platelet stickiness and also result in absorption into the arterial wall.

Four possible interventions

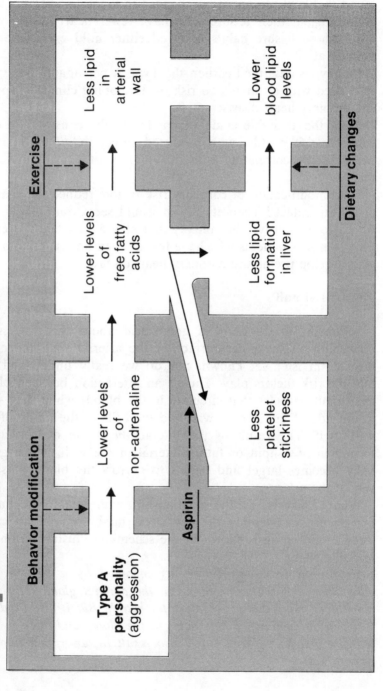

One can slow down the reactions by various interventions, as shown opposite. Behavior modification could, theoretically, favorably alter the sequence of events. Exercise as well as dietary changes could reduce the level of blood lipids. Certain drugs also can inhibit the reactions in several ways. For example, it's known that aspirin will reduce platelet stickiness.

By modifying the risk factors, then, we could act in a variety of ways to interfere with the chemical reactions that ultimately lead to the thickening process in the arterial wall.

It's very interesting to note that, although age-adjusted mortality from coronary heart disease increased by 19% in the United States from 1950 to 1963, it began to decline in 1964 and has continued to decline since. And the rate of decline has accelerated in recent years.

The reduction in mortality between 1963 and 1975 averaged 22%. It may or may not be coincidental that there had been a drop in tobacco consumption by the middle-aged male population and a drop in the consumption of animal fats in the United States over the same period.

There are other factors that may be responsible, too, such as better treatment of high blood pressure, coronary-care units, exercise programs and surgical procedures. In short, it seems prudent for physicians and health authorities to continue to encourage the public to modify the coronary risk factors.

Exercise and heart disease

Until recently, our culture discouraged adults from exercise, and there were good historical reasons for this. Settlers in North America worked very hard physically to make a living from the land. Their descendants tended to migrate to the cities, where one sign of success was an occupation and a style of life that required minimal physical activity. Technology aided this, bringing us the motor car and "labor saving" devices.

Thus, a successful manager of 30 years ago was someone who did not cycle, hike, jog or do strenuous work, either on the job or in his leisure time. Exercise played little or no part in dissipating tension or in coping with stress for the previous two or three generations of urban managers.

Prolonged rest was also a mainstay in the management of many diseases. Tuberculosis was treated with bed rest for months or years. Rheumatic fever was managed by putting the patient to bed for weeks or months until all signs of inflammatory activity had subsided. Surgical patients were kept in bed for two or three weeks after a routine operation such as an appendectomy.

Back then, rest played a very important part in the treatment of heart-attack victims. And the rationale was understandable. A heart attack leaves a softened area that must heal and form a scar, and the process takes several weeks. The less activity there was, the less work the healing heart would be called upon to perform—and patients were kept quiet in bed for seven or eight weeks.

They were shaved, fed, bathed and eased ever so gently onto a bed pan in a manner suggesting that each movement might be the last. The patient's convalescence at home lasted several months. If his job involved physical labor, he was usually advised to leave it. He was encouraged to restrict his recreational pursuits to sedentary hobbies.

If, 30 years ago, the patient asked his physician whether he could play golf, the characteristic reply would be, "Yes,—as long as you don't go at it too strenuously." No advice could be less helpful in restoring a patient to health.

In addition to the historic, cultural attitude toward exercise in general, there seemed to be another very sensible reason for heart-attack victims to avoid physical activity. It was well known, and it still remains one of the hallmarks of coronary heart disease, that the patient may die suddenly—with or without chest pain.

Sudden death occurs, not because the heart has failed as a pump, but because the electrical circuitry that signals the heart to contract becomes scrambled.

The heart then fails to contract effectively, blood no longer circulates, and the brain, which is extremely sensitive to a lack of oxygen in the blood, no longer functions effectively. The patient loses consciousness and dies shortly thereafter.

Sudden death is a dramatic and terrifying event in any situation. It's particularly shocking if it occurs while the victim is physically active. There are few events as frightening as witnessing the unexpected death of someone playing tennis or running to catch a bus.

Thus, three decades ago, it seemed reasonable for middle-aged and elderly people, especially if known to have coronary heart disease, to avoid vigorous or even moderate physical activity. And this attitude was particularly strong among physicians who treated managers. As we came to know later, this approach was not only inappropriate, but the harm done to the middle-aged men of the Western world was incalculable.

At the University of Western Ontario our original interest in cardiac rehabilitation started in 1962 and was focused on two questions:

1. Was it true that exercise placed a middle-aged man with a previous heart attack in jeopardy of having a second attack or of dying suddenly?
2. Was it feasible and safe to increase the physical activity of a selected group of coronary patients?

We really didn't conceive of rehabilitation as a form of treatment, and we certainly had no thought that increased activity might alter the long-term course of the disease. We simply questioned whether it was really necessary to keep all those patients in a psychological strait jacket for the rest of their lives.

From a search of the literature in 1962, as well as our clinical experience, it seemed that there was a slight increase in the likelihood of sudden death if the patient had been habitually sedentary and if the activity involved isometric work, particularly in cold weather.

Isometric activity occurs when a person performs work against resistance, such as lifting heavy objects. Exposure to cold may trigger irregular heart beats. So the bad reputation of shovelling snow, particularly wet and heavy snow, proved to be well founded. This two-way combination of factors is at work when an otherwise sedentary middle-aged or elderly individual shovels snow following the first storm of the winter.

But we wondered whether this meant that *all* men, either healthy or with coronary heart disease, should forego all moderate or vigorous activity for the rest of their lives. It was in this

69

Probability of death in the next 10 years

Males: chances in 100,000 and rank of cause

Cause	30 C†	30 R*	35 C	35 R	40 C	40 R	45 C	45 R	50 C	50 R	55 C	55 R	60 C	60 R
Heart attack	206	3	617	1	1371	1	2653	1	4456	1	6811	1	9945	1
Lung cancer	36	11	95	5	225	4	477	2	905	2	1484	2	2153	2
Motor vehicle accidents	367	1	324	2	315	2	322	3	327	6	330	9	—	—
Cirrhosis of liver	47	7	120	4	225	5	316	4	362	4	390	7	425	10
Stroke	49	6	84	6	156	6	309	5	535	3	931	3	1754	3
Suicide & self-inflicted injury	224	2	269	3	290	3	302	6	316	7	305	10	—	—
Intestinal cancer					107	7	180	7	342	5	533	4	812	5
Heart disease-other forms							131	8	177	11	355	8	644	6
Stomach cancer							121	9	227	9	391	6	633	7
Tumors-cancer							111	10	183	10	297	11	449	8
Chronic bronchitis & emphysema							106	11	263	8	521	5	921	4
Pneumonia							104	12	—		—		—	
All others	683		1000		1501		2132		3021		4383		6055	
All causes	1905		2860		4568		7264		11281		16998		25032	

†Chances *Rank

Prepared by Dr. John H. Howard from Statistics Canada figures, 1971.

setting that we began research in 1963.

Exercise and rehabilitation

It seemed prudent to begin with a few "good-risk" coronary patients, that is, patients who had recovered from their heart attacks without complications and who also seemed psychologically sound. We soon found that this wouldn't be easy. The patients we approached felt very apprehensive at the thought of being trained, and it took a year before four volunteers appeared—who also had their family doctor's approval. Dr. Michael Yuhasz, from the physical-education faculty of Western, undertook to lead that initial training program.

After some preliminary tests, including a standardized two-step test to evaluate fitness, we began a 14-week program of exercises of increasing intensity. There were no major difficulties, and at the end of the experimental period we repeated the tests. Each of the men had increased his cardio-respiratory fitness significantly, and the positive mood changes we observed were dramatic.*

We were impressed with the comments of the four men about their altered reaction to stress. They felt better able to cope with day-to-day stress, and we thought it important to look at the mood changes more closely. With the help of Dr. Alan Paivio of the psychology department of Western and Dr. Barry McPherson, we designed the following experiment.

Two similar groups of post-coronary patients were given a battery of psychological tests to measure emotions such as anxiety, depression, self-confidence, optimism and so forth. We then trained one group over a six-month period. The other group met with the same instructors over a similar period in a setting that featured recreational swimming. The amount of activity was minimal in the control group, the swimmers, and the training effect small.

At the end of the experimental period, we repeated all the psychological tests. We found that both groups showed signifi-

* We reported these early findings to the Inter-American Congress of Cardiology in 1964.

cant positive mood changes, although they were somewhat more pronounced in the trained group. This finding emphasized the powerful, therapeutic effect of putting patients with similar problems together regularly in a setting where improvement might be expected.

This group-therapy effect is, of course, well known. The important point, however, is that it was difficult to isolate the so-called "training effect" as the major contributor to the patients' emotional changes that allowed them to manage stress more effectively. This information was important in shaping the design of more elaborate and more recent studies, as we shall see.

In 1967, the only death during an activity session occurred. At the next session a few days later, we spoke to the men, saying we were very sorry, that we would continue to make the program as safe as possible. One of them interrupted, by saying:

"You don't have to tell us all that. We all know that this can happen. We're sorry it did, but it won't stop us from going on. The program is great and it means a lot to us."

We suddenly realized that the men had come to terms with the incident in a way that we hadn't. We'd learned much over the years from the patients, and the cardiac rehabilitation program now appeared in a different light. Not only did the participants feel better emotionally once they were in the program, but they obviously had faced the possibility of sudden death squarely.

Indeed, it seemed to us that in working out regularly they were symbolically asserting their willingness to accept the consequences of their disease in a positive, not a negative way.

Illness provides a stress the patient may cope with in several ways:

1. He may accommodate the stress by denial. That is, he acts as though the illness hadn't occurred. He doesn't change his way of life, doesn't discuss the illness, and more or less effectively represses the whole experience. This defence can work well for some patients, though no personal growth occurs and his behavior and habits may continue to increase the risk of the disease or its progression. For

example, the individual with cirrhosis of the liver who continues to drink alcohol, or the coronary patient who has high blood pressure and doesn't take his medication and continues to smoke, are both examples of denial.

2. Another way of coping with the stress of an illness is to retreat. This used to be the common response to a heart attack. If the patient lived a cautious life, perhaps retiring prematurely, taking no chances on anything, becoming increasingly dependent on those around him, he would exist in a state of depression, often not easily visible, quietly awaiting and fearing the end. Physicians often used to encourage this response.

3. Still another approach is to use the illness as an opportunity to increase self-awareness—to face one's own mortality directly and to respond to the stress by maturing. The physician should encourage and support this response, because the patient may require much courage, and he'll often need all the help he can get.

It's this third response of personal growth that the cardiac rehabilitation program stimulates effectively. For example, one of the patients who had a heart attack 10 years previously, at age 49, was an executive in a fairly large company. Although he performed well, he didn't like his job and for some years he'd quietly desired to own and run a small business of his own. After his convalescence, he decided: "It's now, or never."

The illness had been a catalyst in his decision. He looked around and within 18 months managed to acquire a book store, which he proceeded to revitalize. Though he worked long hours and perceived considerable stress, it felt different than the managerial stress in his former corporate position.

His sense of job satisfaction was high and, as we've learned from our study of stress in managers, this is about the most effective antidote to job-related stress. Ten years after the heart attack, this individual was well, productive and managing a very successful operation.

By 1971, we'd recorded enough experience to try to see whether our program had any influence on the likelihood of a second heart attack. We compared the recurrence rate among participants in the program with the recurrence rate among similar patients who hadn't been in such a program. We found that the recurrence rate was significantly lower among the exercising patients.

However, this type of retrospective analysis in which the experiment isn't tightly controlled has much room for error. The results did suggest the need for more research. And the outcome was a sophisticated and larger study, in which seven university centres in Ontario recruited patients and began carrying out identical experiments.*

They would compare two similar groups of coronary patients. One group would exercise in a jogging program. The other would play recreational games with less-intense physical activity, but which gave patients beneficial effects of group activity.

The object was to see whether exercise vigorous enough to produce a significant training effect would affect the chances of a second heart attack. The jogging group and the recreational games group were recruited to be as similar as possible: equal numbers of Type A's, equal numbers of individuals with high blood pressure, equal numbers with chest pain on exertion and equal numbers of white- and blue-collar workers. All of the 751 participants were to be followed for four years unless they dropped out of the study and couldn't be traced.

The study hadn't been completed at the time of this writing, but the results to date indicate there's no significant difference in the recurrence and death rate between the jogging group and the recreational-games group. There are several possible explanations for this:

1. It may be that once one has reached middle age, vigorous exercise will not affect cardiovascular outcome.
2. Or it may be that four years isn't long enough to follow a patient in such an experiment.

It could well be that we're dealing with several populations and that only certain patients will have an altered chance of recurrence following exercise. We know of two patients who had clearly defined regression or improvement of their narrowed

---

* The Ontario Exercise-Heart Collaborative Study.

coronary arteries with no change in their lives but an exercise program.

Yet in a very careful study that Dr. Nolewajka, Dr. Kostuk and two of the authors, Dr. Cunningham and Dr. Rechnitzer, completed at the University of Western Ontario, we found no difference in the amount of coronary artery narrowing among patients in the jogging program and those in the light-activity or recreational-games program.

Thus, it's unsettled at present as to whether the intensity of physical activity after a heart attack will prolong life.

That statement seems, however, several light years from the question posed at the beginning of this era, 15 years ago: "Would it be feasible and safe to take a patient who has recovered from a heart attack and restore him to a normal mode of existence with the usual activities of healthy men?"

It's well to remind ourselves that the mechanism by which the coronary arteries become narrowed still isn't clear, and the roles that stress, cigarette smoking, elevated blood cholesterol and so forth play aren't well understood. They have certainly an associational relationship with the disease, but their possible cause-and-effect relationship is still unproven. We do know that, among men who have already sustained a heart attack, those whose blood pressures are kept normal and who discontinue smoking fare significantly better.

When people ask the physician on our team whether exercise prolongs life, Dr. Rechnitzer's answer often depends upon his mood. He has sometimes been heard to say, "I don't know" or "Does psychiatry or religion prolong life?" Less facetiously, we say that survival is a standard and legitimate yardstick to use in measuring an alleged therapeutic effect. Everything else being equal, a treatment that prolongs life usually is better than one that doesn't.

But, after 15 years of studying the effects of exercise on cardiac patients, we've come to know that exercise, as a type of "therapeutic intervention" or treatment, has several aspects not included in most other conventional medical remedies:

1. The patient is an active participant, in every sense, in his own treatment. He's not essentially passive, as in

75

swallowing a pill, receiving an injection or being subjected to an operation.
2. The patient must endure discomfort of his own making with intermittently painful ankles and knees.
3. There's required of him considerable self-discipline, a recently maligned and falsely denigrated virtue.
4. The treatment for some has within it potential esthetic qualities, tangentially, not directly, related to his desease. This last aspect, for some, comes to transcend all others.

Imagine this difference. You're a man of 43, a manager, who suffers a heart attack in 1960, the beginning of the end of the old era. You're told by your physician that the most you can do is return to work with a rest after lunch and a little golf, played carefully. You're a man of 43, a manager, who suffers an identical heart attack in 1970, just 10 years later. Within two years, after entering an intensive exercise-rehabilitation program, you've completed the Boston Marathon, one of the most gruelling, formidable challenges a person can attempt. If you were to ask the 1970 patient, after his marathon run, whether the treatment had been effective and whether it would prolong his life, we're sure he would have a marvellous, free and joyous belly laugh.

Though it seems prosaic to say so, we must so often redis-cover what our ancestors knew, though sometimes in a crucially different context: that physical fatigue can be pleasant, that it's difficult to feel tense or angry after walking 10 or 15 miles and that striving can be healthful if taken in a propitious setting. Striving, just for the fun of it, is exactly what play is. We see play as an activity without ulterior ends in which the partici-pants engage seriously, like five-year-olds, but shortly after the outcome can hardly remember who won. In fact, the outcome is absolutely secondary. What *is* important is the process, the activity itself.

Can Type A's change their ways?

Unfortunately, the urge to play doesn't come easily to one group in society—the Type A's, who seldom waste any of their striving on pointless fun. But must it be so? Once a Type A, always a Type A? Or can a Type A learn to modify his own behavior to benefit his health?

We have no reliable research data in this area, but our own experience leads us to believe that some Type A's can be motivated to change their ways—but only under certain conditions.

If the patient is a Type A_2 (that is, not a full-blown Type A_1 and one who can shift to a Type B_3, given the right surroundings) strong motivation can be successful. Such an individual must look very closely at his own behavior and responses to his environment, particularly at work. He can, we believe, even in middle age, modify his sense of time urgency and the compulsive self-imposed deadlines. However, in most cases the motivation dwindles as the acute event recedes; this, plus deeply ingrained emotional habit and continued exposure to the environment that engenders Type A behavior, conspire to prevent change.

Though we have no experimental data to support this, our observations lead us to believe that within the total Type A population, there's a small subgroup that we would describe as authentic Type A. The authentic Type A has the defined characteristics of the syndrome in childhood, and they're fully developed in adolescence. He operates as a Type A naturally and easily. He remains a pure Type A even when the environment, say on a vacation, would encourage a partial shift to Type B behavior. This individual isn't expressing Type A characteristics in response to his environment; he's a Type A moving through life "with the grain."

We would postulate that this subgroup Type A population isn't at increased risk as far as heart disease is concerned, and that these people remain physically well and vigorous into old age.

But most of the Type A population could be described as Type A "against the grain." These individuals aren't intrinsically Type A, but they learn unconsciously to incorporate Type A characteristics into their behavior. This Type A individual usually moves or reverts in the direction of Type B responses when the environment is modified. This can occur, for example, during an illness when the individual is placed in a gentler setting to recover.

It characteristically happens during a vacation; the individual becomes unaware after a week or so that his sense of time urgency, his need to keep "busy," his pre-occupation with deadlines all fade somewhat and even seem slightly unreal. In short, his *authentic* mode of response starts to emerge.

We believe it's this variation of the Type A personality, in which the acquired style of response really goes "against the grain," that poses a threat to health. On the other hand, we suspect that this is the expression of the Type A syndrome that might be susceptible to behavior modification techniques.

A future chapter will explain how the against-the-grain Type A can *try* to alter his behavior and offset some of its effects.

4. Stress and your performance

About productivity and pressure,
effectiveness and health

ONE of the purposes of this book is to help you understand the
relationship between stress and the long-term effectiveness of
managers. So we should now examine more closely some
aspects of job performance.

Clearly, a manager's personal productivity depends on his
ability to motivate others to work hard. It's a crucial factor. But
what *does* motivate an individual to work hard? The organizational climate? The rewards system? Or his own personality and
attitudes toward society?

Undoubtedly all three contribute to the motivation of most
individuals to some degree. But, as we saw earlier, the majority
of managers run their office lives on the "pressure principle" –
deadlines, tightened schedules, quotas and budgets. Often subtle, and at times intense, the pressure to perform needles, per-
suades, urges and coerces the individual to work.

The reasoning behind the principle is quite simple. A reasonable number of fleas is good for the dog—they keep him busy.
Managers believe that a little anxiety and stress is a good tonic
and a spur to ambition and achievement.

Few will argue with the necessity of having motivational

The vicious feedback of stress without exercise

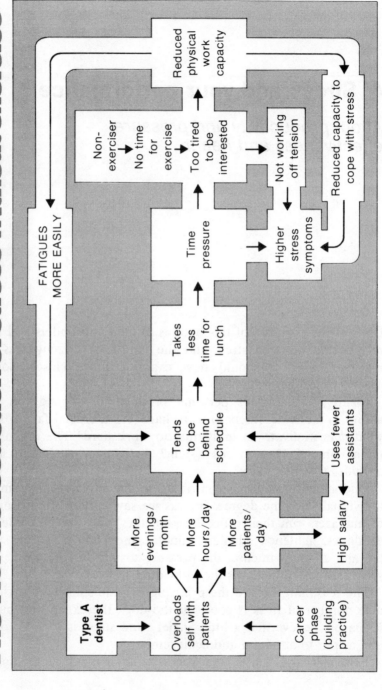

forces and stimuli in our lives. Ask any sky diver or mountain climber. But what is a reasonable number of fleas? And when do interest and excitement become fear and distress, leading to illness and failure?

These are the dangers inherent in the use of the pressure principle in managing people. The number of fleas and how hard they should bite are never defined, nor is it recognized that anxiety may be one man's tonic and another's poison.

In chapter one, we pointed out that there can be too little as well as too much pressure in a manager's life. We termed those with too little pressure the *rustouts* and those with too much the *burnouts*. We also noted that the rustout and the burnout can easily suffer from the same amount of stress. In fact, in most cases, the rustout is a far more serious problem both psychologically and in terms of physical health.

In many cases, the protection the burnouts have is that they often enjoy their job. This job satisfaction has a great capacity to modify the effects of living at an accelerated pace. There's a trap, however, in which the burnouts are often caught. This was revealed in a study we conducted with Ontario dentists.

The study showed that stress in an individual's life is often self-inflicted. It also showed how working under pressure is often related to stress symptoms, fatigue and reduced physical fitness, as the chart opposite spells out clearly.

Our burning out dentist was usually a Type A individual in the active process of building his practice. He worked more hours, saw more patients, and as a result made more money. This type of work environment, self-created, put him continuously behind schedule, allowing him to take less time for lunch and relaxation. This constant sense of time pressure is related to higher stress symptoms.

The same type of dentist is a non-exerciser, either because he has no time to exercise or is too tired to be interested. Because he is a non-exerciser, he has reduced fitness and, at the same time, isn't working off stress and tension. This reduced fitness means he fatigues more easily, and he falls further behind schedule. He's in a cycle where his work pressure reduces his exercise, which reduces his fitness, which makes him fatigue easier, which simply puts him further behind.

Many managers also fall into this trap. When under heavy stress and pressure, the first thing they give up is exercise. The irony is that this is the time they need it most. Active exercise is good preventive medicine when it comes to stress. It helps to combat fatigue when under pressure and helps work off stress.

Exercise has a number of other benefits—and may even be related to productivity. In the study with dentists, we found the best predictor of productivity was a dentist's fitness level. The most fit were also the most productive. This same relationship may hold true for managers, although there's little experimental evidence at the moment. Productivity depends on a number of factors, and one of the most significant is job and career satisfaction.

Job satisfaction vs job pressure

In our research with managers, we examined the relative effects of job pressure and job satisfaction on productivity. The initial results indicated that job satisfaction is more significantly related to productivity. If you want productivity, it's better to build satisfying jobs than exert pressure for performance.

Many managers seem to understand this, but still reach first for the pressure system to increase performance. This is perhaps because it's easier to institute a de-personalized system rather than build satisfying jobs.

The definition of a satisfying job has evolved in recent years. Where the managerial "success ethic" was once characterized by material reward, career advancement, recognition and community status, the new criteria are job satisfaction, meaningful work, good health, domestic tranquility and job security.

This evolution reflects some important changes—in particular, a movement toward a more integrated life in which the issues of work and career are brought into balance with personal fulfillment. As we've already pointed out, it also represents awareness of the personal costs of excessive striving and ambition—costs often counted in terms of health and family problems.

We should also point out, particularly to senior management, that part of the new success ethic is a greater concern with job and financial security. In one recent survey of Canadian managers, 35% of the respondents indicated that during the previous two years their concern with job security had increased. This increasing concern with security had a number of possible sources.

Inflation and the stagnant state of the economy was obviously one. Another is the fact that some Canadian corporations had already started to look at the issue of managerial productivity, and their first reaction had been to reduce the numbers of managers. Also contributing to financial concerns was the threat that managerial salaries might not keep pace with inflation, while managers bargained from little or no collective strength.

Both of these issues have raised the spectre of management unions.

In the Canadian survey just mentioned, 60% of the respondents indicated they would either be interested or very interested in the possibility of joining a collective bargaining unit. In an American survey, also conducted recently, half the managers surveyed favored a change in labor laws that would make managerial unions possible, and one out of three said they would join or consider joining.

The managers saw several advantages in unions: job security, higher wages, better health and fringe benefits. But they noted that collective bargaining wouldn't solve all their problems, especially the disenchantment arising from more subtle conditions in corporate life.

Management productivity

This growing interest in management unions, as part of a general shift in the success ethic, is only one visible factor in a major issue affecting organizations of all sizes. The issue is the productivity of managers and professional staffs.

For some years now, the top echelons in business have watched some puzzling trends taking shape in those middle ranks:

1. The turning down of promotions at a relatively young age —accompanied by an easier readiness to "settle in" and perhaps stagnate.

2. The more thorough and critical look at transfers, along with a greater reluctance to move geographically.
3. Early and unexpected retirements.
4. The general re-evaluation of the success ethic—including the leaning toward management unions.
5. A decline in corporate loyalty and attachment.

Each of these factors is having an effect on management productivity. We often hear the same phenomenon expressed as "lack of motivation and commitment" and "management stagnation" and "the obsolescent manager." It's a growing phenomenon, with important implications for both organizations and individual managers.

In the first place, we must consider the fact that the ranks of managers and professionals are growing, relative to the total organization. In a recent survey among 10 major Canadian companies, eight of those 10 corporations reported that, in the previous five years, management and professionals had grown as a percentage of all employees. In some cases the percentage change was surprising.

In fact, organizations are changing shape—from pyramids to barrels. The coming bulge is in the middle.

The same phenomenon can be seen in terms of salary structure. As a percentage, managers and professionals represent a growing proportion of total salaries.

For wary top management, a combination of higher costs and greater numbers dictates a sense of vigilance. A second factor, however, contributes to the problem.

During the past 25 years or so, corporations have achieved most of their productivity gains at lower levels in the organization. This is where technology has made its principal advances, either in terms of increased outputs or reduced inputs. It's questionable whether companies can make such large gains again at this level. Many processes have become as efficient as they're likely to become, and the incremental gains in productivity still available at the lower levels of the organization may not be worth the cost.

In that case, where will companies go ahunting for productivity gains in the future? At the growing mid-level, of course. The numbers are getting bigger, the costs higher, and at times the need for the services performed may seem questionable.

In short, over the next few years top management will begin to look very carefully at the productivity of the white-collar employee. (In fact, it's interesting to observe that white-collar unemployment already has reached its highest level since the 1900s.)

The great dilemma

The issue of management productivity, however, will soon become a dilemma for the top echelons. What can they do to improve managerial performance at the mid-level? If they do what managers have traditionally done, they'll merely step up the pressure down the line.

And this would happen while the attitude of many in the middle ranks is tending toward less commitment, less striving and a change from traditional career values.

The result? We can forecast a mounting load of stress on many of the individuals concerned — and very possibly a disappointing change in productivity. Excessive pressure might or might not pull a rustout out of stagnation, but, as the charts on pages 86-87 show, it just also might push others over the hump into the low-performance burnout stage.

As the reader has seen, our own research on stress has impressed us by how much better it is for the individual to run too fast rather than too slow. As a result, when making decisions that influence the pressure and tensions of the job, it would seem better to err on the side of too much rather than too little pressure.

This seems like a good general rule, but clearly there are exceptions. For example, merely putting more fleas on a rustout dog, without understanding why he behaves so sluggishly, could be utterly destructive. The toll in illness and death, caused by fear and distress, could be very high indeed.

Must we torture the dog?

Is there a way out of the dilemma? Apart from torturing the

Job pressure and job performance

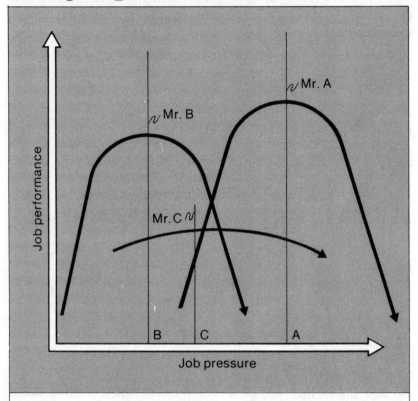

While almost all individuals follow performance curves of the same general shape, unfortunately (for the manager) their curves have different levels and slopes. As we can see clearly above, Mr. A reaches his best performance at higher levels of job pressure than does Mr. B. But Mr. C, on the other hand, shows only small gains in performance for wide changes in job pressure. As pointed out in chapter one, the manager has to "know his men"—that is, know which ones would be more productive with more pressure, and which with less. A manager's productivity depends on this ability.

The rustout and the burnout

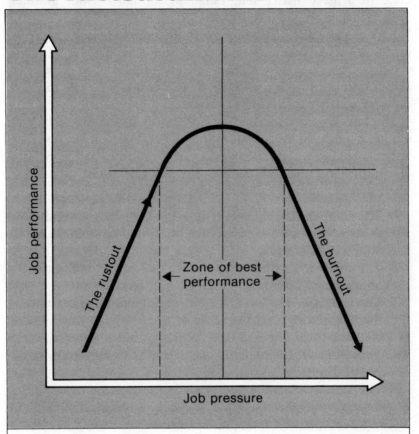

As job pressure increases, performance increases up to a certain point and then declines thereafter. The rustout lacks enough pressure in his job to bring forth his best performance. The burnout has too much pressure, has passed the peak, and has slipped down the performance curve. A manager must learn to live his own business life at the top part of the curve— not too much pressure, not too little. In managing others, the same issue is involved. To get the best productivity from his subordinates, the manager should impose neither too much nor too little stress.

dog with too many fleas that bite too hard, what else could be done to achieve better long-range performance from middle-rank managers?

Let's look at one of the major problems: managerial obsolescence. It's a problem that pressure alone can't solve. This is clearly so because the manager reaches this state, in which his skills no longer match the demands of his job, when he has lost the very capacity to adapt to change.

The responsibility for finding an answer here rests with *both* the individual and the organization, according to work done by Richard Hodgson of the University of Western Ontario's School of Business Administration. We can see why when we understand that the answer involves such issues as these:

1. The company: being sensitive to the fact that, as conditions evolve, the risk of obsolescence of individual skills and abilities increases.
2. The company: being able to make and accept realistic appraisals of individual strengths and weaknesses.
3. The company and the manager: maintaining the capacity, the opportunity, and the sense of responsibility for continued learning and development.
4. The manager: maintaining energizing skills, especially his physical fitness.
5. The manager: maintaining a vigilance over the career opportunities that exist both inside and outside the organization, and even outside his present career.

Another big problem in long-range effectiveness involves motivation. And the pressure principle won't necessarily solve it either. Part of this problem, too, rests with the individual, with his personal values and personal objectives. As we know, many of these are changing. But is a need for achievement still a principal ingredient in the personality of the manager? If so, toward what goals is this motive directed? Have the goals of the corporation become unclear and perhaps meaningless to the individual? Again, both the individual and the company must be involved.

Also involved: the nature of managerial work. Have management jobs become so diluted that they lack the potential to evoke interest and commitment?

By finding answers to these questions, both top brass and individual mid-level managers can attack the long-range effectiveness issue before the situation gets truly serious. We might call this preventive action.

Unfortunately, dealing with a situation that already exists becomes far more difficult. But there is a tool to help untie the knot—a concept that suggests a systematic way to deal with low-performance, low-productivity managers and professionals. It's called "redirection," but few business people understand the term or the ideas behind it.

In a study of 12 major corporations (four in the United States), researchers found that no company had or used a systematic method of "redirecting" managers back into a stage of involvement, commitment and personal growth. In almost every case the solutions were ad hoc and piecemeal, ranging from dismissal or early retirement to nominal promotions.

In short, we were shocked to learn that every organization had failed to systematize ways to "redirect" the inadequately performing manager—even though in the next few years he may well grow into one of the prime bugbears in manpower administration.

The problem of treating non-performance managers is difficult. And the extensions of the problem in terms of morale, productivity, promotional opportunities and the welfare of the individual concerned are obvious. But little practical work has been done to identify and use methods that would fulfill any moral obligation of the organization or attempt to recover the value of its human asset.

It's clear that top management must develop a creative, innovative, systematic approach to the problem, and build it right into the company's manpower administration.

Part of the approach must involve job-change solutions: job enrichment, lateral movements, demotion, firing, early retirement, relocation, career orientation. But part must also involve development programs: skills training, education programs, plus training to achieve behavioral change.

How a company applies such a program, deciding which measures will best suit which specific cases, obviously depends on the nature of each individual situation. The important point is that the *system* itself exists. For one thing, that's what enables the top echelons to diagnose the root cause of each situation in the first place.

Health and effectiveness

One other aspect of his life has a heavy impact on the manager's long-term effectiveness: his health. No matter how suitably skilled and well motivated the manager may otherwise be, sickness can destroy his productivity.

We've seen, in this and past chapters, that many factors in the corporate milieu—excessive or too-little pressure, change, ambition, uncertainty, "driven" behavior—are associated with stress and serious illness. The evidence is indisputable. Now we should again face the by-now familiar question:

Where does the responsibility in this sensitive area lie—with the individual manager or with the corporation?

To begin, we can state flatly that individual managers must assume the responsibility for their own health, by becoming aware of the main contributors to disease and disorder. What is stress? What can it do to your body?

Awareness is the first step, action the second. By reading this book, for example, managers have lifted a foot for that first step —but what about the second?

Until quite recently, many have turned the responsibility over to the physician, hoping that drugs, surgery and the "miracle of medicine" will somehow atone for a history of poor and neglected health habits. It's a bad bet, and many individuals and organizations have begun to recognize the risks.

Two factors have renewed interest in health and fitness. The first is a growing awareness of health and fitness factors as contributors to chronic disease. The second is the visible incidence of illness and premature death that has touched almost every management group. Heart disease, of course, is the number one threat, and most managers know at least one colleague who has had a heart attack before age 60. The individual's concern for health and fitness is obvious.

At this point, enter the corporation, whose reasons for concern are just as compelling. From the corporation's point of view, there are several motives behind a growing interest in health and fitness.

The first is simply humanitarian. If the organization can play a role in the preservation of health and longevity, then it's a responsible and humane thing to do.

The second motive has to do with the performance of managers on the job. There's a general belief that those who are fit are better performers.

On this issue, some people have gone so far as to claim that the best predictor of managerial performance may be physical fitness. (Our study of the dentists tends to support this.)

A third motive involves the corporate risk of having a top manager die or become ill. In these cases, the job responsibility being carried by key managers is difficult, and at times impossible, to shift to other individuals.

Similarly, a fourth motive has to do with the preservation of corporate bench strength. In this case, the risk is in having managers on the second and third teams die, after 30 years in the organization, just before making their most significant contributions. In such a situation, the personal tragedy is obvious, but the corporate tragedy can also be severe. Think of the investment not only in terms of money, but in the development of skills, abilities and knowledge that have been vested in a manager with 30 years' experience.

The preservation of health and fitness is preventive medicine. It protects the organization's most important resource. It maintains and enriches the value of its human assets, and is an important provision for the future success and integrity of the organization.

An organization unconcerned with the health and fitness of its managers isn't concerned enough about its future.

Two recent cases illustrate such issues. In the first, top management in a major service organization became concerned about whether key employees were showing symptoms of intolerance to stress. The whole organization had undergone a structural reshuffle, and had launched a program designed to bridge the gap between field and headquarters personnel. In this case, stress reactions became so visible that top echelons simply had to make changes.

The second study involved a large financial institution whose bench strength was being seriously depleted by the ravages of coronary heart disease.

In both cases, management began asking these questions:

— Was the incidence of heart disease higher in their organization than in the normal working population?
— Were specific policies or procedures of the organization responsible for the problem? Which ones?
— What preventive action could be taken to alleviate the problem?

Cases like these (and there are many) have sharpened the debate about where the responsibility for managers' health lies. One view holds that health and fitness are personal factors and, consequently, the sole responsibility of the individual. Others argue that work and health are necessarily the concern of the organization.

The authors have observed that the first point of view prevails at lower levels of the organization, except in cases where employees are involved in some readily apparent occupational hazard. The second seems to be more prevalent at middle and senior management levels. Here, the importance of the individual's role in the corporation is seen as justifying organizational concern for health and fitness. Annual company-paid medicals for top managers are an excellent example of this concern.

Obviously, both managers and the company share some responsibility. Poor fitness and health can be prevented to a large extent, and the organization can play a number of roles in this process. Possibilities range from simple encouragement to the provision of programs and facilities for employees.

However, we must emphasize that the individual maintains the primary role in this process. Only he can, for example, lower his cholesterol level, maintain his weight, stop smoking and consult a physician about his blood pressure.

In short, the principal responsibility for his own health and fitness will always rest with the individual. In the next two chapters, we'll examine ways to help him uphold that responsibility.

5. Exercise and your body

About fitness and disease,
how-to's and how-not's

THIS CHAPTER is about physical exercise—what it can and can't do for you, how and when you should use it in your personal stress-management program.

In chapter three we explained the role of exercise in the rehabilitation of cardiac patients. Here, however, we'll concentrate on the role of exercise among managers who haven't suffered heart disease—and don't want to.

To begin, we must point out again that recent research confirms a fairly strong association between physical inactivity and coronary heart disease. Two reports, both mentioned briefly in chapter three, are typical of the kind of scientific evidence that supports this link.

One, done by Dr. Morris and his co-workers in England after a study of 16,882 male executives aged 40 to 64, observed a significantly lower incidence of coronary heart disease in men who engaged in active leisure pursuits. The leisure activities weren't necessarily very strenuous activities; for the most part, they would be classified as moderately intense—gardening, do-it-yourself projects, keep-fit programs and walking or jogging faster than four miles per hour.

Among men who reported involvement in these active leisure pursuits, the relative risk of developing coronary disease was about one third of that among men not involved in such activities. In addition, the involvement in such active pursuits apparently protected against a rapidly fatal heart attack.

That is, among those men who were active and who did have a heart attack, the chances for survival were about four times better than among those men who were sedentary in their leisure time. The researchers offer no explanation as to why the active men appeared to be protected. But it's evident that only the most active men were so protected, and therefore one might argue that the protective mechanism works through the training of the cardiovascular system. In this case a lowered exercise heart rate would reflect the higher state of the fitness of the active group.

In similar research reported two years after the British paper, Dr. Paffenbarger and colleagues studied 6,351 longshoremen who worked in the San Francisco Bay area. The study followed these men for 22 years or to age 75 to assess levels of continual physical exertion in relation to risk of fatal heart attack.

Again, as in the previous study, those men engaged in the most vigorous activities were protected.

In this case it was activity on the job and not in leisure pursuits that was important. The high-activity group engaged in on-the-job activities that were similar in intensity to the leisure activities of men of the most active group reported in the British study. The intensity was greater than five kilocalories per minute or close to the four-miles-an-hour walking speed. Men doing such jobs had a mortality rate from coronary heart disease about half of that among those doing less active jobs. And the protective nature of such activity extended to the sudden-death syndrome; again, men in the most active jobs had a sudden-death rate one-third that of men in less active pursuits.

These studies and other work in the field make important points that, at the risk of boring the reader, we'll emphasize again. Namely: Physical activity of sufficient intensity—walking or running faster than four miles per hour, or the equivalent—apparently results in a degree of protection against heart disease. In addition, when active men do suffer heart attacks, their chance of survival seems to be three or four times better than that of their sedentary friends.

But can't exercise enlarge your heart?

Some observers have related frequent and vigorous physical activity over many years to the development of an enlarged heart, so-called athlete's heart. Those who worry about this problem claim that this enlarged heart size is related to future heart disease. In fact, there's no evidence to support this position.

Conditions that require an increased force of contraction over long periods of time may result in hypertrophy, or enlargement. In the case of the heart, hypertrophy results in an increased muscle mass capable of developing more total force. Many factors may lead to hypertrophy in the heart muscle, or myocardium. These include constriction of the aorta; renal or systemic hypertension; damage to valves of the heart; chronically reduced oxygen supply, or hypoxia; and possibly severe prolonged exercise.

But there are important differences between the causes. If exercise causes an enlarged heart muscle, it's related to a stress associated with an increased demand for oxygen by the tissues for periods of time considered sufficient by the person. In cases of disease, the enlarged heart muscle is related to stress caused by some problem within the system, and the person has no control over the duration.

We must also point out that the enlarged heart may exist in two different states: hypertrophied, and hypertrophied *with failure*. The former may result from vigorous exercise, and it leads to a heart with an increased pumping capacity. The athlete's heart has a greater cardiac reserve, and is capable of providing more oxygen to the tissues at maximal work loads. The latter results from disease—a chronic volume or pressure overload on the heart—and it results eventually in a state in which the heart fails to pump blood adequately.

In recent studies conducted at our laboratory we've observed that a program of endurance training, running or jogging over a six-month period is associated with marked improvements in fitness, but no changes in the thickness of the myocardium or enlargement of the heart chambers. We performed these studies with a relatively new research and diagnostic tool that permits us to "look" at the heart by passing sound waves to the organ and then recording the graphic images formed by the echo. By analyzing this echocardiogram, we can measure various aspects of the heart, including heart size and the thickness of the heart muscle.

Our results, which didn't show an enlarged muscle after six months of training, may be inadequate because of the shortness of the training period. But this was the longest reported study of the training of middle-aged men where echocardiography has been used to analyze heart changes. And these findings are consistent with several echocardiographic studies of endurance athletes (men who had experienced a lifetime of activity).

Other scientists who have studied athletes from several different sports have suggested that the heart-muscle thickness may be substantially increased only in those who participate regularly in high-resistance anaerobic activities such as wrestling or weight-lifting—activities seldom taken up by middle-aged men and women.

There also may be an interaction between age and the changes that take place in the heart. Studies of young rats exposed to a program of endurance swimming showed a large increase in heart weight. Virtually all time-period studies of training and human cardiac dimensions have used adults as subjects, and, since none have reported the development of true myocardial hypertrophy, it may be that the larger hearts of endurance athletes result from training prior to maturity. Studies of young swimmers (five to 17 years) have reported cardiac enlargement that wasn't pathological in nature. It remains to be seen whether hypertrophy could be developed in young children who take part in a program of endurance exercises over several months or a year.

We emphasize that the slightly enlarged heart of an adult endurance athlete isn't the result of a pathological condition and isn't considered a problem. There's no evidence to indicate any enlargement of the hearts of middle-aged men who take part in an endurance training program of up to six months, and there's little enlargement in long-time adult athletes. The slightly larger hearts of the endurance athletes probably stem from exercise prior to maturity.

Don't people drop dead from exercise?

Death from coronary artery disease during exercise, although not frequent, does occur often enough that it makes headlines.

Then, who writes about the man who dies from heart disease in his sleep?

The current popularity of running and jogging may have resulted in some people exercising too hard and without an adequate warm-up period. It's true that vigorous exercise can precipitate a fatal heart attack—if the weakness is present in the heart of the victim. But consider that Dr. Kenneth Cooper, of the Institute of Aerobic Research, has exercised more than 5,000 joggers with *no* fatal heart attacks.

Although there may be many causes for an exercise-induced heart attack, the problem should be avoided with adequate safety measures. You'll find the general rules for starting an exercise program later in this chapter. Briefly, they include a proper medical evaluation with a stress test, and then a very gradual and moderately increasing exercise program. You don't need to get out of breath while jogging. If you can't talk while jogging, you may be going too fast.

What about when people grow older?

With increasing age, there's apparently a reduction in the intensity of physical activity on the job and a drop in the amount of leisure activity. Physical fitness (as measured by such factors as maximal oxygen uptake) also decreases with age. The two factors may be closely associated, although the decline in the fitness of the heart with age may result from a general aging phenomenon quite distinct from the reduction in activity. In short, there's some concern that the elderly in general don't spend enough energy on activity to sustain an optimal level of cardiovascular fitness.

We usually associate aging with unfavorable changes in physiology and health. Measurements such as physical work capacity, maximal values of oxygen uptake, ventilation and muscle strength, to mention a few, decline with age.

Yet it has been found that general exercise or specific endurance or weight-training programs often delay the onset of these age-related changes—and may even result in favorable changes in the opposite direction.

In comparison with sedentary controls, active, elderly individuals generally have more efficient cardio-respiratory systems both at rest and during exercise, a greater capacity to do physical work and more favorable body compositions.

Physical activity may also be important in preventive medicine for the elderly. One report indicated a *tenfold* increase in the mortality rate of non-exercisers aged 65 to 69 years compared with men of the same age who exercised regularly. The mortality rate was five times greater among the non-exercisers in the 60-64-year-old age range.

Furthermore, physical inactivity has been associated with a higher incidence of various diseases, whereas physical activity or exercise can reduce the incidence or diminish the severity of pre-existing diseases. These results are by no means conclusive, but they do suggest that an active life style in the elderly goes hand in hand with good health.

Some studies have attempted to analyze the relationship between physical activity and the psychological state of the elderly. Researchers have observed that physical activity is related to an improved sense of well-being and a general state of alertness. It's obvious, however, that they cannot say whether the general psychological well-being encouraged the active life style or whether the activity promoted good health.

Retirement brings a sudden major change of life style. Men and women often find themselves with little to do and become less and less active. Whether increased activity during this period of change would help to combat the problems observed isn't clear. A program of regular physical activity at retirement has been observed to ameliorate the usual downward trend at this time of life. The usual increase in body fat and decrease in leg musculature was stopped in those retirees who were active during the first year off the job. Improved life satisfaction and self-esteem scores have been measured in retirees who had remained physically active.

In general, though, we don't understand this area of concern too well. While we do know that retirement is a time of increased prevalence of disease and disability, we don't know much about the role of activity or lack of activity. With the trend toward early retirement and the large bulge of adults in the population moving toward retirement, this certainly will be a major problem of the future.

Changes occur throughout every person's life in terms of health and physical activity. We know that physical fitness or cardiovascular fitness increases gradually up until age 12 to 14 in women, and until about age 18 in men—and afterwards there's a slow and steady decline. Physical training will tend to slow down this aging trend. In fact, very active 60-year-old men have been observed to have fitness levels superior to those of less-active 20-year-olds.

Maximal heart rate also declines with age, at a rate equal to about 220 beats per minute minus the individual's age. Since, as we've already pointed out, activity also declines with age, there may be a direct relationship between these two factors. In general, the trainability of older persons also is reduced, and with any given training program you should expect a smaller percentage improvement with older persons.

Must you start young?

Exercise habits established early in a person's life appear to be critically important to old-age life habits—and in particular to the ability of the older person to respond favorably to a program of endurance exercise. Persons exposed since childhood to a life of general physical activity appear to respond quickly to programs of endurance exercise in adult years.

Small laboratory animals, exposed for the first time to vigorous physical activity in their adult years, have shown that the results of such a life without activity in the growth years can be disastrous.

In these experiments the male animals actually failed to adjust to exercise begun so late in life; they lost weight rapidly, and some died. It should be noted that the female animals managed to survive, and showed some improvement in their fitness.

Our knowledge about the physical fitness of children is to a great extent a recent development. Exercise training in young children hasn't been well studied, but there appears to be no worry that exercise can damage their health. As long as the child is normal, vigorous physical activity appears to be a positive stressor. Improvement in the fitness of children with training varies with their initial fitness levels. As in most age ranges, you can expect a 10% to 20% improvement with a vigorous exercise program.

One question of keen interest to those involved in physical activity: "What's my individual potential for vigorous activity?" To some extent your genetic makeup sets this limit, but general activity levels also are important. Studies involving a number of identical and fraternal twins discovered that the basic fitness levels of the identical twins was much closer than that of the fraternal twins, although all the subjects appeared to have had similar environmental influences.

To a large extent, the basic level of cardiovascular fitness is set genetically. Olympic athletes are essentially born with this potential capacity—but training accounts for at least 30% of their physical ability.

We've also learned that young children who need physical activity the most will, if given the choice, opt out of it. In other words, if schools permit young boys and girls to decline physical education, those with the lowest levels of fitness won't take the activity classes. On the other hand, the fit elect to remain active. (We might question the wisdom of allowing youth too much freedom in this regard.)

Do the active live longer?

We don't know whether you can expect to live longer because of a lifetime of sports or other physical activity. Studies to find out whether successful athletes at school or college can expect to live longer than those sedentary in early life have shown that, on average, young athletes cannot expect to live any longer than their sedentary companions. Usually it's hard to find lifelong addicts to participant sports, so a full life of physical activity is hard to evaluate. Old men have competed in marathons, but that proves little. We're sure, however, that an active life style will permit the older man or woman to outperform younger sedentary individuals.*

In short, there's no good evidence that regular exercise will increase your life in years, but it can enhance the quality of your years.

Exercise and weight control

Endurance exercises over long periods of time can markedly reduce the total body-fat content. Experiments have shown that the reduction in body fatness in exercising young rats has resulted in a decrease in both the size and number of fat cells. This has important implications for human beings.

During growth periods before puberty, fat accumulates in various locations in the body, noticeably under the surface of the skin. This fat accumulation results from an increase in both the number and size of fat cells. But at some point in growth the fat-cell number becomes fixed. That is, if the body stores more fat it does so with an increase in the fat-cell size but not in the number of fat cells. In short, the bodies of adult animals and humans appear to have a fixed number of fat cells and they store fat by increasing the fat-cell size.

Exercise appears to play a very important role in the development of fat deposits. If young children perform regular exercise, the fat-cell division in their adipose tissue is retarded—and this reduces the potential for obesity in early years. Furthermore, if a young person engages in regular exercise, it reduces the number of fat cells in his body at maturity, and adult obesity is less prevalent. If, however, the child is sedentary and gains weight, the deposit of fat ensues and both fat-cell size and number

---

* Some people still believe the athletic or mesomorphic body build might be a detractor from longevity, while the lean linear body of the ectomorph might give him an advantage. This is a generalization unsupported by scientific evidence; very little is actually known about the relationship between a person's body build and his health.

increase. At maturity the young adult will have more fat cells and the potential for development of obesity will increase.

Thus, early-life exposure to exercise may be critical to the ability of the adult to maintain a low percentage of body weight as fat.

We've shown that exercise also reduces the fat content of adults' bodies. In a recent study we conducted with a group of women, we observed marked increases of fitness (34%) with nine weeks of training. During this period we observed little change in total body weight, but body fatness dropped by 10%. This decrease in fatness clearly showed itself in smaller girth measurements—a most pleasing result for the participants.

Parents can do their children a life-long service by encouraging them to exercise; it will keep their childhood body weight low and, more important, curtail the development of fat-cell numbers. For the reasons we've just examined, sedentary children will tend to put on weight and may be obese in adult years. And as adults they may find it very difficult, if not impossible, to lose this weight. Remember, too, that exercise by normal healthy adults will help to reduce their fat weight and usually their total body weight as well.

Exercise and low back pain

One of the very common complaints of middle-aged persons is a non-specific pain in the small of the back. One must treat this problem with caution. The pain may result from an injury to the lower spine or from a disc that has become protruded or is diseased, thereby placing pressure on a nerve.

Once a physician has eliminated the possibility of such injury with a thorough physical examination, we find that the cause of low back pain is more often than not muscle strain. This strain might result from a specific act, such as lifting a heavy object, but we can usually trace it to inadequate exercise of the abdominal muscles.

If you allow the stomach muscles to become too weak, it will result in a slight rotation of the pelvis. In this case, the hip will rotate slightly. The lower back muscles then must do much of the work in holding the upper body erect.

A sensible program of stomach exercises should always be part of any good exercise program. You can do many exercises involving strength development (and some of these will be outlined later), but the development and maintenance of adequate stomach strength is very important for optimal health. Stomach exercises are essentially simple in nature, requiring a mild overload or resistance to the stomach muscles.

The problem with some stomach exercises is that the individual starts out on a program too vigorously. Any set of exercises for strength development requires a slow approach, and this is most important in stomach exercises.

To begin, lie on your back, arms at your side, your knees bent with both feet flat on the floor. Slowly lift your head and shoulders until your head is clear of the floor. After several days of this exercise, you can then proceed to raise your head and shoulders until your head touches your knees. Eventually you can do this with your hands clasped behind your head.

When you can do about 30 or 40 such sit-ups a day, there's probably no need for additional stomach-muscle exercises. But you can do a useful isometric exercise for the stomach right at your desk; maximal contraction of the stomach muscles while sitting helps to strengthen them.

Exercise and hypertension

Hypertension, or high blood pressure, has become a very troubling disease in North America. (It's estimated to afflict about 22 million Americans.) The big problem with the disease is that in more than 75% of the cases there's no apparent physiological reason for the problem. High blood pressure, if untreated, can lead to other, more obvious problems such as coronary heart disease and kidney disease.

Blood pressure is the force with which the blood is pushed through the systemic circulation. If this pressure increases, it places an added strain on other essential organs such as the kidneys.

In comparison with the research work done on regular physical activity and coronary heart disease, little has been done with patients suffering from hypertension. And there's still considera-

103

ble controversy about the effects of exercise on hypertension; any statements made on this topic are subject to argument.

One leading research authority in this field has stated that an analysis of available data will reveal that physical activity in those with arterial hypertension will result in a lower blood-pressure level both at rest and during physical exercise. Others have studied the problem by looking at populations engaged in different levels of physical activity.

The increase in blood pressure with age, reported by many researchers, has been observed to be lower in more active groups such as the more primitive populations of less developed areas of the world. A summary of many studies of population activity and hypertension indicates that, although all population studies are not consistent, the lower blood pressures are found in the more active workers.

Body fatness may be a compounding factor in these studies, since the less-active persons were also the fattest. One study found no difference in blood pressure between those employees starting as clerks and those starting in more active work in the same company. The clerks, however, had higher blood pressures later in life. This suggested that the differences observed in blood pressure later in life were due to the level of physical activity of the job sustained over many years.

In summary, most observations indicate that men with less-active jobs have a greater incidence of hypertension than those in more-active occupations. We can say, then, that physical inactivity appears to be related to hypertension although the relationship is possibly weaker than with other factors such as salt intake—a dietary item many nutritionists think to be the major cause of hypertension.

Certainly, a more active life style plus a considerably reduced salt intake could go far in reducing the incidence of hypertension in our society.

The hypertensive patient must be very cautious in starting a program of exercise—and the type of exercise is also very important. The patient should start very slowly, concentrating on low-resistance exercises such as walking; he should avoid any resistance exercise such as weight lifting or isometric work. Shoveling snow is a good example of the type of daily activity to avoid. The general exercise program will be detailed later in this chapter.

Exercise in the heat

Exercise in the heat can carry with it some risks, particularly for the novice. This area of research has received a lot of interest since the late 1960s. The interest undoubtedly came in part from the health problems associated with such exercise.

Marathon running races, which have become popular, may also expose participants to problems of heat stress. In fact, it's probably true to say that the only serious health threat to the well-conditioned marathoner is a fatal heat stroke. The major problem in heat stress and physical activity appears to be the less-than-adequate intake of water during or before the activity.

Everyone exercising in the heat should have access to water. And you should swallow it; don't merely swish the water around your mouth and spit it out.

You should also take note of some very good hot-weather recommendations recently published for marathon runners. Although the marathon is a very demánding event, not likely to be taken up by most readers of this book, the guidelines are worth following in less vigorous physical activity in the heat:

— In very vigorous sports, such as the marathon,
  temperatures above 25°C (77°F) can be dangerous. If the
  temperature tops 28°C (84°F), the event should be called
  off. (It's not a bad idea for the novice to cease strenuous
  physical activity lasting 30 minutes in 26°C heat—or at
  least slow right down.)
— Adequate amounts of water should be available at all
  times.
— Exercisers should be warned against dehydration and
  encouraged to drink at least a cupful of water every 20
  minutes.
— Everyone associated with a hot-weather event should know
  the signs and symptoms of heat stroke.
— Proper medical facilities should be at hand.
— Any abnormal behavior in hot weather should be treated
  immediately.

For most novice exercisers, heat stroke is unlikely—but the chance exists. When it's hot: slow down, drink plenty of water, and, if too hot, don't exercise.

Exercise in the cold

Those of us who live uncomfortably close to the earth's poles must run and jog in very nasty weather much of each year; a severe winter can be particularly discouraging for the jogger. Yet, if you're to maintain an effective exercise program, you can't stop activity for three, four or five months of the year.

You'll find that by exercising out-of-doors throughout the year you can slowly acclimatize yourself to the changing seasons as they come. As you exercise through the autumn into winter you tend to notice the weather changes less. We think that to start an exercise program in the winter would be much harder than in more pleasant weather conditions.

The major consideration in cold-weather exercise is proper clothing, but it's surprising how few clothes you need if the activity is vigorous, even on the coldest of days. When the temperature drops to $-10°C$ ($+14°F$) or below, it will feel very cold. If the wind is gentle, however, it doesn't take long before there's a warm layer of air next to the skin and you'll actually begin to sweat.

We usually recommend good-quality shoes with a good jogging suit, or old pants and sweater, gloves and hat. If the wind is heavy, a light nylon shell is useful. Be careful with the nylon shell; it's possible to build up moisture under the clothing which can cause a chill, especially if you stop exercising outside for too long.

If the outdoor activity is less vigorous, you'll need heavier clothes. Outdoor walks require much heavier clothes. Cross-country skiing presents some problems, particularly at the start of a season. In this case you may wish to dress as in jogging, but your skill level may dictate a slower pace—and therefore heavier clothes. Heavier clothes early in the season; lighter clothes as skill and fitness develop later in the season: that's possibly the best cross-country rule. Often it's a good idea to take along a backpack with a nylon jacket, in case it turns cold or you wish to stop skiing for some time.

Your personal exercise program

By now you might be convinced that science has shown a positive relationship between physical inactivity and ill health, especially of the cardiovascular system. If so, how can you begin to exercise in a way that you'll find enjoyable and beneficial? There are many prescribed formulas for exercise programs. These recipes are very useful and can meet the needs of many people, but often they're too specific. Many people can't accommodate easily to such specialized prescriptions.

We propose to outline for you the ingredients that are basic to all good exercise programs. These basics are applicable whether the participants are Olympic athletes or beginners, very young or very old. The four main factors of any exercise prescription are: (a) intensity, (b) duration, (c) frequency and (d) type of activity.

Intensity

The intensity of the exercise program is governed by several factors, which include your individual feeling of well-being during the exercise sessions, but which can be expressed more objectively in other ways.

The first step in developing the intensity level of any exercise program is to have your physical fitness established by a standard exercise test. This test is often done by your physician as part of a general physical examination prior to starting a program of endurance exercises. The exercise test can be done in several ways—on a stationary cycle ergometer, on a bench step-up test or on a motor-driven treadmill.

Each of these exercise modes has its advantages and disadvantages. It would be unusual to find a treadmill used, unless you attended a large testing centre, although the treadmill has some obvious advantages over the others. The exercise, walking or running on the treadmill, is a natural one. The exercise intensity, governed by the speed or slope of the mill, can be held constant or varied very precisely by the operators. The individual taking the test can't "beat the machine" by walking slower. This means the operator can be sure of the test's accuracy. In addition, the exercise test (walking or running) is similar to normal activities.

The cycle ergometer (a stationary "bicycle") is also a very useful exercise tool. The pedaling rate is usually controlled by a metronome, although some ergometers don't require the pedal rate to be controlled. The pedal rate is standardized, because that's how testers determine the power output of the task.

In a step-up test, you step up to and down from a step 10 to 30 centimeters high, with the stepping rate set to a metronome. As in the cycle test, the stepping rate is critical in determining power output.

In these ways the testers determine your maximal working capacity—by estimate in most cases. The specialists then set the exercise intensity at a level sufficiently high to improve your fitness, but not so high as to be a danger to your health. The intensity must be set greater than about 40% of one's capacity to result in any improvement in physical fitness. It's usually sufficient at about 60% to 80% of your maximal work capacity.

Actually, the fitter you are to start with, the greater the percentage of your capacity that can be used in exercise. In the early phases of any program, the intensity should be kept as low as possible—usually starting at about 60% and after six months to a year gradually increasing to 80%. Remember, this increase is compounded by the fact that your maximal work capacity also increases as you increase the relative intensity.

Specialists can set the speed of walking or running by the exercise test, but they usually establish a specific heart rate and use it to determine the training intensity. In this procedure maximal heart rates are determined to a great extent by age, and can be approximated by the following equation:

$$\text{Maximal heart rate} = 220 - \text{age (in years)}$$

If you're 40 years of age, your maximal heart rate would be close to 180 beats per minute. You can get a good approximation of the training heart rate by subtracting your age from 180 beats per minute. In the case of a 40-year-old, this would be 140 beats. That is, at the end of the training session your heart rate should be 140 beats per minute. This heart rate can, of course, be determined more accurately from the test on the cycle ergometer.

Frequency

The exercise frequency is of less importance than the intensity, although it takes two sessions each week to maintain fitness and three or more to see an improvement in fitness. There's a plateau in fitness improvement when you increase the training frequency beyond three times per week. We have no information on the fitness effect of training more than five times a week. But the frequency of training would be related to the energy expenditure, therefore to the caloric expenditure—and to weight loss.

Duration

The duration of training is particularly important for fatties, since the distance covered is more critical than speed for the loss of weight. We see little weight loss when the programs call for fewer than three daily sessions per week and fewer than 20 minutes per session. The total amount of work done per session is also critical for fitness development, as long as the intensity is high enough, as described earlier.

There's good evidence that fitness improvement will be similar for activities performed at a lower intensity and longer duration compared to higher intensity and shorter duration—as long as the total work done in the two programs is the same. Although programs of at least 20 to 30 minutes are critical for weight loss, the health problems associated with the feet and knees will increase with exercise duration, especially in the early phases of a program. It's essential, therefore, that during the first four to six weeks of running the duration should be increased slowly from an initial 10 minutes to the 20 to 30 minutes.

The speed of progress will depend upon how well you feel. Always respond to the aches and pains by slowing down the progress. Remember that too much haste over the first months of an exercise program may result in sore muscles and joints, which could keep you from your program over a much longer period of time.

Type

The mode of exercise isn't too important as long as the activity is low-resistance and repetitive in nature. Walking, running or jogging, skipping, swimming and cross-country skiing are good examples. These activities contrast with very low-intensity activities such as golf (which has little value unless the subject is very sedentary or he jogs between strokes) or bowling. On the other hand, the novice wishing to improve his fitness should avoid high-intensity activities such as weight lifting.

Any activity will do quite well, as long as it is low in intensity (60% of maximum) and carried out for 20 minutes or more.

Age has little effect on the ability to increase fitness, given the provisos discussed earlier in this chapter. In any case, older individuals will take longer to increase their working intensity and duration than younger people.

In summary: It's necessary to train three times a week or more, at more than 40% of your maximal capacity, for at least 10 minutes per session, to realize a training effect. If weight loss is important, the exercise sessions should be as long as possible (30 minutes or more), with intensity kept as low as possible (close to the 40%).

Specificity of training

A very common phenomenon known as the specificity of training, experienced by most exercisers, can cause some confusion in understanding the development of physical fitness.

Specificity of training is that part of a training program that results in physical adaptation unique to the particular program undertaken. For example, we can all see that the results of a program of weight lifting will have results quite different from the outcome of a program of endurance jogging. One will develop strength in the exercised muscles, while the other will result primarily in an improvement in muscular endurance.

What isn't so evident is that the adaptive response to jogging is quite different from that observed in swimming or bicycle riding. All three result in the development of endurance fitness, but there is in each a degree of training specific to the actual exercise. If you want to improve your ability to bicycle long distances, then bicycle long distances; don't swim or jog, even though there's a certain degree of commonality among all three exercises.

We often experience the specificity of training when after several months of jogging we decide to play a game of tennis. We mightn't experience any great respiratory fatigue, but we do have sore muscles for several days afterwards.

The specificity of training has been studied in a scientific setting as well. A group of men were trained for several months, half on a bicyle ergometer and half running. The fitness of both groups was measured on a treadmill and on a cycle ergo-meter. It was found that those who trained with running showed significant improvements in fitness on both the treadmill and the cycle ergometer, whereas those who cycled for exercise showed improvement on the cycle ergometer only.

A training program appears to produce adaptive responses in the heart and lungs as well as the local muscles. The central or heart-lung adaptation appears to be general to all endurance exercise programs, while the muscular or local changes are specific. It's these local changes that dictate the specificity of the training response. In the case of running, the training is more general than the response to bicycling, therefore the improve-ments due to the exercise program are observed both running and cycling.

But remember that it's the general exercise of the heart that counts.

With any low-resistance exercise such as jogging or bicycling, you can exchange a minimum of time for improved fitness—and very probably some definite benefits in health. Research indi-cates that you'll get a degree of protection against heart disease, a slight lowering of blood pressure, a general sense of well-being and a zest for life.

Three half-hour periods a week can have significant results. (There are 336 half-hour opportunities in a week, and surely you can find three for exercise.) Be careful and progress slowly.

6. Stress and success

*About habits and change,
antidotes and "inoculation"*

ONE THREAD runs through all the prime causes of stress in our lives, and specifically in our working lives. The astute reader has probably realized by now that the common filament is *change*.

The links between the phenomena we've examined in this book are complex, but they can be traced. Change, for example, immediately suggests the threat of personal obsolescence—and thus job dissatisfaction and stress. Ambition, so often accompanied by Type A behavior, is a powerful desire to achieve personal change. We also know that Type A behavior seems to flourish in high-growth organizations. And what is growth but a corporate form of desired change?

Certain kinds of external (and possibly undesired) change—intense business competition, economic and social upheavals and so forth—put pressure on the organization itself. And when an organization comes under pressure, so do its people. Too much pressure on, say, an unmotivated or obsolescent rustout can have stressful and tragic results.

To live full and healthy and therefore *effective* lives, then, we must cope with change as a stress-producing force. And, perhaps also not surprisingly, we must learn to cope with the stress of too little of it, as well as of too much.

Either extreme, too high a rate of change or too low, can cause serious problems. We can see why clearly when we isolate the four job situations shown to be closely associated with stress:

Uncertainty and ambiguity

Usually associated with *high* amounts of change, this situation means that job responsibilities aren't clear and the information needed to do the job is either confusing or unavailable. The manager isn't sure what's expected of him, and often he feels he lacks the authority needed to carry out his responsibilities.

Furthermore, he feels the opportunities for advancement and fulfillment are unclear, and he doesn't know how higher management is evaluating his performance. The type of individual who encounters uncertainty and ambiguity is usually both ambitious and productive.

Locked in

The type of manager who falls into this trap feels locked into his job or organization because of his own inadequacies or the lack of opportunity elsewhere. He feels frustrated and stymied, and there's *little* opportunity for change.

Stagnation

Like the locked-in situation, stagnation is associated with *too little* rather than too much change. The manager usually has been in his present job and location for a long time, and has seen very little change in his own or his boss's influence over the past few years.

Conflict and confrontation

Usually associated with *many* changes, the type of job in which this situation is encountered is characterized by heavy

113

workloads and conflicting demands. It usually involves supervisory responsibility for a number of subordinates, and the manager feels he's constantly in competition with others, either inside or outside the organization.

The links between job and change seem perfectly clear. And perhaps no research better depicts the relationship between change and health than the work we looked at in chapter one. You'll recall that researchers developed a scale of common life events and ranked the events in terms of their relative amounts of change and stress. They found that those people high on experiencing change were much more prone to illness and disease.

Ordinary life events, whether pleasant or unpleasant, controllable or uncontrollable, carry a burden of stress. Obviously, pleasant and controllable events are less stressful, but both require adaptation—and adaptation means stress. The accumulation of "change events" over a period of time increases the probability of disease because coping with it lowers resistance. The resulting illness tends to lag behind the change experience by several months.

This research stands as a lesson in human limitations. It should continue to remind us that each of us has only so much energy, and that if we use it up in continually adapting to change, then it's not available to combat illness and disease. In the future, we'll need to be more aware of, and more sensitive to, the psycho-physiological burden of our goals and activities.

Emphasis on health habits

In our studies, the authors of this book have found that the five most effective techniques used by managers for reducing stress symptoms are these:

1. Build resistance by regular sleep, exercise and good health habits.
2. Compartmentalize life into clearly defined work and non-work segments.
3. Let no other activity interfere with regular physical exercise.

4. Talk problems through with peers on the job.
5. Withdraw physically from the situation.

You can't help but note the emphasis on good health and exercise habits. The value of such habits was further demonstrated recently by Dr. Lester Breslow in a five-and-a-half-year study involving 7,000 people. The seven habits studied were: eight hours' sleep per day; breakfast every morning; no snacks; maintaining weight within limits; no smoking; moderate alcohol consumption; moderate exercise.

Dr. Breslow found that, at age 45, those following six or seven of these habits had an additional life expectancy of 33.1 years, while those at 45 following three or less of the habits had an additional life expectancy of only 21.6 years. That's almost a 12-year difference in life expectancy at age 45 based on some very simple health habits. Dr. Breslow also found the effect to be cumulative: the more health habits you follow, the better your health.

Perhaps a brief comment on each of the health habits and other techniques is in order.

Eight hours of sleep.
Most people need about eight hours of sleep. Some people need a little more, some people a little less, but on average people need about eight. The best way to tell how much sleep you need is how rested you feel when you awaken. If you feel rested with six hours of sleep, that's probably all you need. As you grow older, you need less sleep; the normal range of sleep that most people need is between six and nine hours.

Breakfast every morning.
Breakfast tends to be an important meal in the day, because the metabolic processes of the body have been at rest during the night and some food energy is helpful in getting the day started. Some people do miss a meal during the day, and lunch would seem to be the best meal to miss. If you exercise at noon hour, this helps to decrease your appetite, and, consequently, helps to control your calorie intake both by reducing the amount of food consumed and by expending calories.

No snacks.

This isn't because snacks per se are bad, although most have little or no nutritional value, but people who snack a lot usually have poor dietary habits in general.

Maintain your weight within limits.

There are a number of causes of death linked very closely with weight. Each of us should try to keep body weight within an ideal range. More important than our total weight, however, is the amount of fat we carry. The ideal amount of body fat is 20% or less for women and 14% or less for men. We should, in fact, be concerned about being over fat rather than overweight. Many clinics can tell you what your body fat percentage is.

No smoking.

The health hazards associated with cigarette smoking are very firmly established. There's little doubt that heavy users of cigarettes have a shorter life expectancy. The risks associated with pipe and cigar smoking, while not healthy habits, tend to be minimal—unless the smoke is inhaled.

Moderate alcohol consumption.

Again, the risks associated with excess alcohol consumption are well documented. In the Breslow study, one drink of hard liquor per day (or the equivalent alcohol content of other beverages) or less was considered moderate.

Moderate exercise.

We have covered the importance of exercise and fitness earlier in the book. Perhaps the word moderate should be emphasized. If you're just starting an exercise program, begin slowly and gradually improve. Too strenuous an exercise program, rather than helping with stress, can simply become another stressor in your life.

It's interesting that simply following good health habits is one of the best techniques for dealing with stress. Perhaps this simply reflects a preventive concern which, as in most things that have to do with our health, is usually more therapeutic than trying to cope after the fact. A good personal preventive program is a better intervention than dealing with stress-related illnesses once they develop.

Compartmentalize your life into clearly defined work and non-work segments.

In addition to following good health habits, managers who seem to deal effectively with stress also separate their work and non-work lives. They work hard on the job, but at home they're able to blank out job problems. We suggest that you can work as hard and as long as you want at the office, provided you don't take the load home.

Talk problems through with peers on the job.

One manager told us that if we wanted to help with the stress in his life, we could simply help to solve some of his work problems that were creating it. One's peers on the job often have the capacity to do this. It's interesting that we found, in the same sense, that talking problems through with one's spouse didn't seem to be an effective technique. It would seem that, while your spouse often can be an empathetic and sympathetic listener, he or she usually doesn't have the capacity to help solve stressful work problems.

Withdraw physically from the situation.

The technique of temporarily withdrawing physically from the stressful situation also seemed to be effective. Just get away from it for awhile, take a break. When things are really getting tense, go for a walk in the plant or around the block. Physical withdrawal, in fact, seems to work better than trying to switch tracks mentally. We've found that dropping what you're doing and taking up another unrelated task doesn't seem to be very effective.

There always remains for managers the question of how much of the stress in their lives is self-inflicted—often a consequence of their own behavior. The Type A syndrome is an excellent example. In this regard, a capacity for constructive introspection along with a few techniques based on clinical experience may be of help.

Combatting Type A Behavior

As mentioned earlier, Type A individuals seem to run a particular risk of developing coronary heart disease. The dilemma for the manager, of course, is that organizations often reward Type A behavior highly. Type A's do get things done.

We also believe that Type A behavior is predominantly environmentally determined. That is, the arrangement of rewards and contingencies in the individual's job and career is the factor most apt to produce Type A behavior. As mentioned earlier, there are probably a few "natural" or "with the grain" Type A's, but most individuals are heavily influenced by the expectations and reward systems in organization life. Consequently, it becomes particularly difficult for the manager to change Type A behavior. He faces a stimulus embedded in the work environment, and his learned and rewarded response patterns become natural and habitual reactions.

What can the Type A do to somehow allay the risks associated with this behavioral syndrome?

The first thing the type A's should do is keep the traditional coronary risk factors in the normal range. They should know their blood pressure, cholesterol and triglyceride levels, have them checked annually, and keep them under control. They should reduce or stop cigarette smoking. They should maintain their weight within the ideal range, and keep themselves fit by regular and adequate exercise. All of us, of course, should do the best we can on these issues, but it's particularly important for the Type A's.

Next, the Type A must realize that Type B people are not necessarily unproductive. They can be as productive as Type A's. What most characterizes the Type A's is the *constant* sense of hurriedness, the *constant* sense of time urgency that continuously pervades their life. Type B's get ahead by being more creative, more innovative and using better judgment. Type A's usually get ahead simply by working harder.

What the Type A has to do is learn to modify the *constant* and chronic hurriedness and time urgency in his life. He has to learn to live by the calendar not the stop watch. He can begin to do this by slowing down internally, doing some re-engineer-

ing on his life, and by modifying some of the work habits that
are often habitual and strongly indicative of Type A behavior.

Slowing down internally

Type A's are constantly trying to do more and more in less
and less time. They have no time to enjoy life because they're
often busy and preoccupied with getting things worth having.
The Type A never gives himself enough time to enjoy what he
has accomplished. Accomplishment leads only to the next challenge.

Life becomes a collection of experiences. And while, from the
outside, the Type A life often seems glamorous and exciting, it's
often devoid of meaning. Recognition of this fact later in life is
part of the tragedy in Type A behavior.

Slowing down internally helps to provide the opportunity to
enjoy your accomplishments. It also provides the opportunity
for creativity, innovation and some time for reflection on those
things in life of true value.

It's difficult to slow managers down because their jobs are
usually characterized by "much work at an unrelenting pace"
and because productiveness is often mistakenly equated with
simply working harder. In this same sense, however, the manager can work hard, be productive and not be a Type A. What
he must do is understand that it's the *constant* sense of time
urgency, the *constant* sense of hurriedness that's critical to this
behavioral syndrome.

Here are a few thoughts on how one can modify a pervading
sense of hurriedness by trying to slow down internally:

*1. Try to stop doing more than one thing at a time. Discontinue
polyphasic thinking.*

Individuals often develop interesting personal and work habits that stem from a constant sense of hurriedness:

— Dictating while driving.
— Talking on the phone, listening to a subordinate and
  scribbling a memo, all at the same time.
— Shaving while on the john.

119

— Watching television, listening to one's spouse and reading the evening paper, all at the same time.

The same phenomenon applies to the thinking process. A Type A man shaving in the morning will often consider—all at once—what he'll have for breakfast, what route he'll take to work, where he'll park his car and what he'll do first when he gets to the office.

When you catch yourself doing these things, remind yourself that they portray that sense of hurriedness you're carrying with you. Generally, try to do more things in series and fewer in parallel.

2. Learn to listen without interrupting.

Try to learn to be a good listener, not someone just waiting to talk. The minds of Type A's are usually racing and their impatience often makes them poor listeners who interrupt and race ahead to fill in the conversation. When you find yourself filling in another person's story before he's finished, pause, relax, try to control your impatience.

3. Do things that require concentration—not just the trivial.

Type A's are always looking for the condensed version—the executive summary. Over time, they tend to lose the capacity to concentrate or stay with a single problem for a period of time. Superficiality, then, can become a characteristic of their thinking and their work.

So read something other than newspapers and condensed news magazines—something difficult but worthwhile. Maintain your capacity to concentrate. Be concerned about detail and, consequently, your ability to understand complex problems.

4. Learn to savor your food; take time to enjoy it.

Many Type A's put eating in the same category as refuelling the car. Learn to savor your food. Make dining a sensuous experience. Meals can be an excellent time for relaxation—a period in the day to take some of the hurriedness out of your life, to balance things out. It's also a good psychological transition zone, a period you can use to make the transition of thoughts and feelings from work to home and family and vice-versa.

5. Cultivate your sense of humor.

Extreme Type A's are usually very serious people. They often lose their capacity to laugh, to see the humor in small things. They're usually working so hard that they miss the small moments of joy often crucial to continued good health. Laughter is a great tonic.

6. Review once a week the causes of your "hurry sickness." Are you really rushing anywhere?

Sit back once in a while and ask yourself why you're in such a hurry and whether things are really happening faster because of it. We've all seen drivers who continuously change lanes, cutting in and out of traffic in an attempt to get ahead faster. You usually meet them waiting at the next stop light. All that dodging and weaving usually gets them nothing. Ask yourself once in a while whether the hurriedness in your own life isn't producing the same results.

7. Remind yourself that you tend to be quick tempered. Control your impatience.

Type A's tend to carry with them a lot of repressed hostility that often breaks through to the surface and explodes. Their sense of hurriedness leads to impatience, which, when repressed, converts to hostility. Short exploding tempers are not uncommon among Type A's.

8. Take time to show your thanks and appreciation to others in a genuine way.

People always in a hurry usually fail to be genuine in their expressions of thanks and appreciation. Their expressions of thanks or goodwill often seem ritualistic, canned or a little phoney. In the same way, they usually have trouble finding time to consolidate their acquaintances and friendships. These things are important in life and are often the victims of a constant sense of hurriedness.

There are ways other than speed to measure your progress.

Re-engineering your life

Type A's should also try to do a little re-engineering on their patterns of living. Here are a few suggestions:

1. Get up earlier, start the day leisurely, don't begin it with a fight against time.
For a Type A, the day will speed up fast enough once he enters the office. To begin the day by rushing through breakfast then rushing through traffic doesn't seem to be prudent. Beginning the day at a little more leisurely pace has the potential to help take the hurriedness out of the remainder of the day's activities. If you don't use a racer's start in the morning, the rest of the day might not feel like a race.

2. Try to find a period in the day for total body relaxation. Noon hour is best.
It's useful for individuals with stressful occupations to have a period in each day that provides at least the opportunity for relaxation. Some relax by exercising (the relaxed feeling usually occurs after the exercise), some do it by meditating, and some do it by quietly reading. For those whose jobs are especially stressful, a period such as this at noon hour would provide both a period for relaxation and an opportunity to balance out the morning and afternoon activities. Noon hour activities, to help break up the day, seem especially useful—but such a period any time during the day is of value.

3. Restructure trips and vacations.
Plan your travelling in a way that doesn't create extra pressure, especially when you're likely to encounter unexpected delays. Go half a day early. In the same way, don't structure a lot of hurriedness into your vacations. Going to Europe for 14 days to "visit" 14 countries is certainly Type A behavior. You may actually enjoy such a vacation, but it doesn't count as rest and relaxation. It still has that sense of hurriedness. One doesn't need to be inactive on a vacation—simply unhurried.

These things, like so many other aspects of daily life, lie totally within your personal control.

Modifying your work habits

In a similar fashion, Type A's should try to modify some of their work habits. Here are a few ideas:

1. Work hard to shed events, instead of trying to do more and more in less and less time. Ask yourself what there is you should stop doing.
Managers usually make rational, objective decisions about what they're going to start doing, but seldom make a decision about stopping any of their activities. Sit down, look at your normal daily activities and ask yourself if there isn't something there you should stop doing. Managers are constantly piling on, but seldom unpiling.

2. Don't leave half-completed projects all over your office; they simply remind you that you're behind.
If the first sight you encounter in your office in the morning is piles of uncompleted work, the resultant response is usually an immediate sense of pressure. File it all away and keep a list in order of priority of what you have to do. When you arrive at work, examine the list and start on priority one.

3. Eliminate business luncheons where possible; take a break to meet with yourself—and exercise.
Are all those business lunches really necessary?
If you do business during lunch, you are not giving yourself a break between the morning and afternoon activities. For some individuals, business lunches can be important if not critical. If you can't eliminate them, try to keep them to a minimum. Noon hour, as mentioned earlier, is often the best time to exercise. An exercise session with business associates at noon is a healthier activity than a business lunch.

Having a meeting with yourself once a day also is a good idea. Managers seem to be constantly in or going to meetings. Once a day for 20 minutes close your door, shut off your phone, put your feet up, tell your secretary you're not to be disturbed, and have a meeting with yourself. Use the time to relax, reflect on problems and consider priorities.

4. Try not to see every situation as a challenge.

A manager is exposed to many opportunities and many problems. If you consider every one of them a challenge to your skills and abilities, you're bound to be overloaded. Don't solve the problem of deciding what you're going to do, and not going to do, by doing them all. You have the capacity to say no. Making good decisions is part of the essence of being a good manager. Deciding to do everything is usually not a good decision.

5. Tell yourself no enterprise ever failed because it was executed too slowly, too well. Cultivate good judgment and decision—not mere speed.

There are, of course, times in the life of a manager when quickness of response is critical to a successful outcome. The problem with Type A's is that every problem begins to fall in this category. In reality, in most businesses there aren't all that many decisions that *have to* be made in great haste; there are just a lot of Type A's making them in great haste. What a successful business needs is the right decision, not the fast one.

6. Control your impatience; don't interfere unduly with people who work more slowly; try not to project your sense of time urgency on others.

Type A's have a great capacity to project their sense of time urgency on other people. While at times this can be a very desirable managerial skill, it can be counter-productive if it becomes the essence of your management style. Because of their constant impatience and hurriedness, Type A's can be particularly irritating to subordinates. They do, in fact, often make others uncomfortable. Good managers don't make other people uncomfortable. It's concern for *both* people and productivity that makes a manager successful.

7. Examine your telephone habits; they're often a good indicator of the Type A syndrome.

Except for people who have jobs or occupations in which the telephone is absolutely critical (stockbrokers, for example), answering every phone call can make you very unproductive. It also can be an indication of a sense of insecurity. Don't let the telephone be the mechanism that schedules how you're going to use the time of the day. If possible, be able to shut off the bell and let your secretary take calls.

There would seem to be a certain Pavlovian conditioning associated with responding to every ring of the bell. Keep control of both the pace and content of your work day. Don't let technology push you around. Technology travels at the speed of light. Don't try to keep up.

These are just a few examples of how you can think about your own Type A behavior. The essence of it all is that hurriedness and activity are not usually good substitutes for productiveness. Don't be trapped by activity alone. Be in conscious control of your own life.

The organization's responsibility

But what of the organization's responsibility for the stress of change in your life, and for your health and fitness—your capacity to cope with that stress?

Although the primary responsibility for your health rests with you, as emphasized in chapter four, nevertheless the organization should have a very real and direct interest in the matter. Given that people are an organization's most important resource, then this resource should be monitored just as other corporate assets are.

In fact, for some years now "human-resource accounting," as a top-management tool, has tried to address this issue. The idea has been to give the top echelons a number of measures (attitude scores, absenteeism and turnover statistics, and so forth) that indicate the effects job conditions may be having on the employees' well-being.

The underlying premise is that, because there's little information available, top management usually doesn't understand the human costs of certain policies and procedures. As a result, the top echelons fail to take into account the "full costs" of specific decisions. So it's the task of human-resource accounting to bring all the hidden human costs out into the open.

Over more than half a decade, the authors of this book have

conducted a continuing series of studies on stress among managerial and professional people. One outcome of our study is a testing, evaluation and feedback procedure designed to inform the individual manager of his fitness level and cardiovascular risk.

Measuring cardiovascular risk

The procedure is simple, and it requires about two hours of the manager's time. It involves these steps:

— Completion of a questionnaire.
— A half-hour interview.
— Taking a blood sample after a 12-hour fast.
— Measurement of blood pressure.
— Taking an exercise electrocardiogram.
— A cycle ergometer exercise test.
— Simple weight and body fat determination.

We give the results and conclusions to the participant in the form of a computer printout. A sample printout, dealing with a male in the 40-49 age bracket, appears in its entirety on the opposite and following pages.

The primary risk factors, shown in part one of the printout, are those known to be the most significantly related to coronary heart disease.* On each factor we give the participant his current value and his previous value. This assumes that he has been tested annually, and it allows him to see changes that have occurred in the past year.

In addition, we provide an age/sex mean value—the normal population value for people of similar age and sex. We also provide a recommended value. The printout then shows three risk criteria (normal risk, some risk, high risk) on each factor, giving the decision rules being used. The individual's value is then scored on these criteria.

Parts two and three of the printout show the secondary fac-

---

* Blood pressure; cholesterol; triglycerides; smoking; heredity; electrocardiograph record; diabetes.

Sample printout of a personal fitness appraisal and cardiovascular risk evaluation

I. Primary risk factors

PERSONAL FITNESS APPRAISAL
AND CARDIOVASCULAR RISK EVALUATION

PARTICIPANT NC. 26003 PRINTED DATE 16-DEC-76
NAME A.N.EXAMPLE SEX/AGE CATEGORY MALE/40-49

I. PRIMARY RISK FACTORS –	CURRENT VALUE	PREV. VALUE	AGE-SEX MEAN	RECOMM. VALUE	–RISK FACTOR CRITERIA– NORMAL RISK	SOME RISK	HIGH RISK	YOUR RISK SCORE NORMAL RISK	SOME RISK	HIGH RISK
A. BLOOD PRESSURE (1) SYSTOLIC	124	124	129	120	120 – 140	141 – 160	160 UP	X		
(2) DIASTOLIC	86	86	81	80	80 – 90	91 – 95	95 UP	X		
B. CHOLESTEROL LEVEL	171	171	*****	200 OR LESS	180 – 220	221 – 260	261 UP	X		
C. TRIGLYCERIDE LEVEL	127	127	****	150 OR LESS	150 – 250	251 – 400	400 UP	X		
D. SMOKING HABITS	0	0	*****	NO SMOKING	NON-USER	UNDER 10 CIG'S OR PIPE, CIGARS	OVER 10 CIG'S DAILY	X		
E. CORONARY HISTORY AND HEREDITY	NO	NO			NEITHER PARENT	1 OR 2 PARENTS AFTER AGE 65	PARENTS BEFORE 65 OR SELF	X		
F. ECG RECORD	TYP	TYP			TYPICAL	OTHER	L.V.P.	X		
G. DIABETES	NO	NO			NO CLOSE RELATIVE		SELF	X		
H. BLOOD GLUCOSE	0	*****								
TOTAL PRIMARY RISK FACTORS							TOTALS	8	0	0

II. Secondary risk factors

II. SECONDARY RISK FACTORS–	CURRENT VALUE	PREV. VALUE	AGE-SEX MEAN	RECOMM. VALUE	–RISK FACTOR CRITERIA– NORMAL RISK	SOME RISK	HIGH RISK	YOUR RISK SCORE NORMAL RISK	SOME RISK	HIGH RISK
A. BEHAVIOR TYPE	A2	A2	NA	B3,B4	B3,B4	A2	A1		X	
B. SERUM URIC ACID	7.1	7.1		LESS THAN 7	7 – 8.0	8.1 – 9.0	9.1 UP	X		
C. WEIGHT (KG) (LBS)	79.3 175	79.3 175		75.1 166	NA	NA	NA			
(1) PERCENT OVERWEIGHT	5.6	5.6		LESS THAN 14						
(2) PERCENT BODY FAT	16.9	16.9			15 – 24.5	24.5 – 29.0	29 UP	X		
D. PHYSICAL ACTIVITY	NO	NO			SOME OCCUPN AND SOME LEISURE	LITTLE OCCUPN AND LITTLE LEISURE	LITTLE OCCUPN AND NO LEISURE			X
E. CARDIO-RESPIRATORY FITNESS (MAXIMUM OXYGEN UPTAKE–PRED.) (FITNESS)	29.44	29.44	36-43	36-43	36+	31-35	LESS THAN 30			X
TOTAL SECONDARY RISK FACTORS							TOTALS	2	1	2

III. Stress indicators.

III. STRESS INDICATORS-	CURRENT VALUE	PREV. VALUE	AGE-SEX MEAN	RECOMM. VALUE	NORMAL RISK	-RISK FACTOR CRITERIA- SOME RISK	HIGH RISK	YOUR RISK NORMAL RISK	SCORE SOME RISK	HIGH RISK
A. STRESS SYMPTOMS REPORTED	4	4			0	1 - 3	4 UP			X
B. LIFE CHANGE EVENTS	8	8			0 - 8	9 - 12	12 UP	X		
C. JOB SATISFACTION SCORE	175	175			224 UP	192 - 223	0 - 191			X
TOTAL STRESS INDICATORS							TOTALS	1	0	2

Summary-overall risk evaluation

SUMMARY-

IV. OVERALL RISK EVALUATION-(TOTALS)	NORMAL RISK	SOME RISK	HIGH RISK
I. PRIMARY RISK FACTORS (TOTAL)	8	0	0
II. SECONDARY RISK FACTORS (TOTALS)	2	1	2
III. STRESS INDICATORS (TOTALS)	1	0	2
OVERALL TOTAL	11	1	4

**** INDICATES VALUES WERE NOT AVAILABLE

Comments

COMMENTS

RECOMMENDED EXERCISE

BASED ON YOUR CARDIO-RESPIRATORY FITNESS MEASUREMENTS, WE RECOMMEND THAT YOU BEGIN AN EXERCISE TRAINING PROGRAM IN WHICH YOUR POST-EXERCISE HEART RATE IS BETWEEN 129 AND 133 BEATS PER MINUTE. THE PROGRAM SHOULD BE CARRIED OUT 3 TIMES PER WEEK DURING THE FIRST 6 WEEKS AND THEN AT LEAST 4 TIMES PER WEEK AS TRAINING PROGRESSES. DURING THE INITIAL PHASES OF TRAINING, YOU SHOULD SPEND 15 MINUTES PER SESSION. AS YOUR FITNESS PROGRESSES, THIS SHOULD BE INCREASED TO 30 MINUTES (ABOUT 2 MONTHS AFTER STARTING THE PROGRAM). IF YOU DECIDE TO EXERCISE WITH A RUN/WALK PROGRAM, YOU SHOULD COVER ABOUT 2.4 MILES IN 30 MINUTES IN ORDER TO GIVE THE APPROPRIATE TRAINING HEART RATE. IN ORDER TO MONITOR THE TRAINING HEART RATE, TAKE YOUR PULSE FOR 10 SECONDS (X6) FOR THE FIRST 10 SECONDS FOLLOWING YOUR EXERCISE SESSION.

CORONARY HEART DISEASE RISK

STATISTICS SHOW THAT   MALES IN YOUR AGE CATEGORY WHO HAVE A SYSTOLIC BLOOD PRESSURE OF 124,A CHOLESTEROL LEVEL OF 171, WHO SMOKE 0 CIGARETTES PER DAY, WHO HAVE A NEGATIVE ECG RECORD AND WHO ARE NON-DIABETIC, HAVE 1 CHANCES OUT OF 100 OF DEVELOPING CORONARY HEART DISEASE IN THE NEXT SIX YEARS.(REF. FRAMINGHAM STUDY)
IF YOUR BLOOD PRESSURE, CHOLESTEROL, AND SMOKING ARE REDUCED TO THE ABOVE RECOMMENDED VALUES, THE RISK WOULD BE REDUCED TO 1 CHANCES OUT OF 100. IF YOUR VALUES ARE LESS THAN THE RECOMMENDED VALUES, YOU HAVE A NORMAL OR LOWER RISK OF CORONARY HEART DISEASE.
THE RESULTS OF OUR TESTING ALSO SHOW THAT YOUR PREDICTED MAXIMUM OXYGEN UPTAKE(ITEM II E) VALUE OF 29.4 IS IN THE LOW RANGE. THIS IS A MEASURE OF FITNESS AND IS CLOSELY RELATED TO YOUR EXERCISE HABITS. WE WOULD RECOMMEND THAT YOU GET MORE EXERCISE AND THAT YOU CONSULT A FITNESS PROFESSIONAL AND YOUR PHYSICIAN ON HOW THIS CAN BEST BE ACCOMPLISHED.

Historical trends

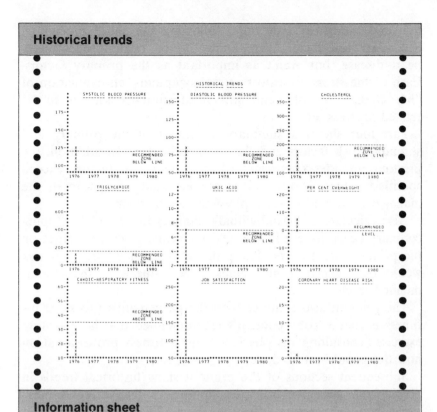

Information sheet

BLOOD PRESSURE

YOUR DIASTOLIC BLOOD PRESSURE IS THE PRESSURE OF YOUR BLOOD DURING THE PERIOD OF THE HEART CYCLE WHEN BOTH VENTRICLES OF THE HEART RECEIVE BLOOD FROM THEIR RESPECTIVE AURICLES; HENCE DO NOT THEMSELVES CONTRACT. YOUR SYSTOLIC BLOOD PRESSURE IS THE PRESSURE OF YOUR BLOOD DURING THE TIME THE HEART CONTRACTS. BLOOD PRESSURE READINGS CAN VARY SIGNIFICANTLY FROM ONE TIME TO ANOTHER.

CHOLESTEROL

CHOLESTEROL IS A FATTY SUBSTANCE WHICH IS PRESENT IN VARIOUS FOODS WE EAT AND IS ALSO MANUFACTURED BY OUR BODIES. IT CIRCULATES IN THE BLOOD AND NORMALLY IS AT A LEVEL OF 180-335 MGM PER CENT. A SIGNIFICANT INCREASE IN BLOOD CHOLESTEROL IS FREQUENTLY ASSOCIATED WITH AN INCREASE IN THE INCIDENCE OF CORONARY HEART DISEASE AND SO HAS BEEN CALLED A CORONARY RISK FACTOR. IF ELEVATED, IT CAN BE REDUCED BY DIETARY CHANGES AND IF NECESSARY BY CERTAIN DRUGS.

TRIGLYCERIDES

TRIGLYCERIDES ARE ALSO BLOOD LIPIDS OR FATTY SUBSTANCES WHICH THE BODY TRANSPORTS FROM THE INTESTINE AND WHICH ARE ALSO MANUFACTURED IN THE LIVER. SIGNIFICANT INCREASE BEYOND THE NORMAL RANGE 50-150 MGM PER CENT HAS ALSO BEEN CORRELATED WITH AN INCREASE IN THE INCIDENCE OF CORONARY HEART DISEASE. IF THE ELEVATION IS MODEST, SIMPLE WEIGHT REDUCTION TO A NORMAL WEIGHT WILL BRING THE LEVELS DOWN TO NORMAL. MORE MARKED ELEVATION OF THE TRIGLYCERIDES E.G. ABOVE 450 MGM PER CENT WILL LIKELY REQUIRE SPECIAL DIETARY CHANGES AND SOMETIMES MEDICATION TO REDUCE THE LEVELS.

CARDIO-RESPIRATORY FITNESS(MAXIMUM OXYGEN UPTAKE)

THIS IS A MEASURE OF YOUR CARDIO-RESPIRATORY FITNESS. IT IS CALCULATED ON THE EXERCISE BICYCLE. IN MANY WAYS THE AMOUNT OF ENERGY YOU HAVE AVAILABLE TO DO WORK IS A DIRECT FUNCTION OF THE EFFICIENCY OF YOUR CARDIO-RESPIRATORY SYSTEM IN TRANSPORTING OXYGEN. YOUR CARDIO-RESPIRATORY FITNESS IS THE BEST OVERALL MEASURE OF YOUR PHYSICAL FITNESS AND IS CLOSELY RELATED TO YOUR EXERCISE HABITS.

JOB SATISFACTION

AS A RESULT OF THE QUESTIONNAIRE DATA WE ARE ABLE TO MEASURE THE SATISFACTION YOU FEEL WITH REGARD TO YOUR JOB AND YOUR CAREER. FEELINGS OF JOB SATISFACTION HAVE BEEN SHOWN TO BE RELATED TO STRESS LEVELS. IN ADDITION, IN A RECENT 15 YEAR LONGITUDINAL STUDY IT WAS FOUND THAT JOB SATISFACTION WAS THE BEST OF A NUMBER OF POSSIBLE PREDICTORS OF LONGEVITY. WE HAVE RECORDED YOUR JOB SATISFACTION SCORE AND THE 'RISK FACTOR CRITERIA' INDICATES ITS RELATIVE RELATIONSHIP TO OTHER INDIVIDUALS IN MANAGEMENT JOBS.

BEHAVIOUR TYPE

FOLLOWING THE FRIEDMAN AND ROSENMAN CLASSIFICATION EACH RESPONDENT HAS BEEN CLASSIFIED AS TO BEHAVIOR TYPE. FOUR POSSIBLE CATEGORIES EXIST - TYPE A1, TYPE A2, TYPE B3 AND TYPE B4. TYPE A BEHAVIOR INCLUDES BOTH TYPE A1 AND TYPE A2. TYPE A BEHAVIOR HAS BEEN DESCRIBED AS FOLLOWS-"IT IS A SPECIAL, WELL DEFINED PATTERN OF BEHAVIOR MARKED BY A COMPELLING SENSE OF TIME URGENCY-HURRY SICKNESS-AGGRESSIVENESS AND COMPETITIVENESS, USUALLY COMBINED WITH A MARKED AMOUNT OF FREE FLOATING HOSTILITY. TYPE A'S ENGAGE IN A CHRONIC, CONTINUOUS STRUGGLE AGAINST CIRCUMSTANCES, AGAINST OTHERS, AGAINST THEMSELVES." TYPE B'S, IN CONTRAST, TEND NOT TO HAVE THESE ACCENTUATED TRAITS.

TYPE A BEHAVIOR HAS BEEN FOUND TO BE SIGNIFICANTLY RELATED TO CORONARY HEART DISEASE, ESPECIALLY AMONG THE EXTREME TYPE A'S.

FOR MORE DETAIL WE SUGGEST YOU READ 'TYPE A BEHAVIOR AND YOUR HEART' BY DRS. MEYER FRIEDMAN AND RAY ROSENMAN, ALFRED A. KNOPF, NEW YORK, 1974.

BLOOD URIC ACID

BLOOD URIC ACID ELEVATION I.E. 8.0 MGM PER CENT IS ALSO ASSOCIATED, THOUGH LESS STRONGLY, WITH AN INCREASED INCIDENCE OF CORONARY HEART DISEASE AS WELL AS WITH AN INCREASED INCIDENCE OF GOUT.

STRESS SYMPTOMS

THE STRESS SYMPTOMS ARE FROM A LIST OF SYMPTOMS INCLUDED IN THE ORIGINAL QUESTIONNAIRE. WE HAVE SIMPLY RECORDED THE NUMBER OF SYMPTOMS YOU REPORTED. THE SYMPTOM CHECKLIST IS A COMPOSITE LIST CONSTRUCTED WITH REFERENCE TO PREVIOUS RESEARCH ON STRESS SYMPTOMS. IN PREVIOUS WORK WE HAVE USED THE LIST AS AN EFFECTIVE INDICATOR OF STRESS BY BOTH THE SIMPLE ADDITION OF THE NUMBER OF STRESS SYMPTOMS REPORTED AND BY THE IDENTIFICATION OF HEALTH FACTORS USING FACTOR-ANALYTIC TECHNIQUES. ON THIS COMPUTER OUTPUT A SIMPLE ADDITION OF THE NUMBER OF STRESS SYMPTOMS REPORTED IS USED AS AN INDICATOR OF STRESS LEVELS.

LIFE CHANGE EVENTS

THE AMOUNT OF CHANGE AN INDIVIDUAL HAS RECENTLY EXPERIENCED IN HIS LIFE HAS BEEN SHOWN TO BE AN EFFECTIVE PREDICTOR OF STRESS AND ITS CONSEQUENT ILLNESS AND DISEASE. THE SCALE WE HAVE USED IS THAT DEVELOPED BY DRS. HOLMES, MASUDA AND RAHE AT THE UNIVERSITY OF WASHINGTON. THE MORE LIFE CHANGE EVENTS AN INDIVIDUAL EXPERIENCES IN A GIVEN PERIOD OF TIME THE MORE LIKELY HE IS TO DEVELOP ILLNESS AND DISEASE. THE LIFE CHANGE EVENTS RECORDED ARE THOSE YOU REPORTED ON THE QUESTIONNAIRE.

tors and the stress indicators, following the same procedure. Secondary risk factors* are known to be related to coronary heart disease, but aren't as important as the primary factors. Each of the stress indicators—stress symptoms, an evaluation of "life change" events, and job satisfaction—is known to be related to stress levels.

Part four shows a summary statement of the primary and secondary risk factors and the stress indicators. In addition, the printout provides comments when certain risk factors exceed specified values. If the values are elevated or abnormal, the manager is advised to see a physician about them.

Also calculated: the individual's chances in 100 of developing coronary heart disease in the next six years, given his values on the primary risk factors. The program also shows how his risk would be reduced if his values were reduced to the recommended levels.

The printout also comments on the participant's fitness. If his fitness is found to be poor, it's recommended that he get more exercise—consulting his physician and a fitness professional on how this could best be done.

Subsequent sections of the printout show historical trends in graph form and give brief descriptions of the variables measured and the factors affecting them. The information also includes references, should the individual wish to learn more about the variables.

"Inoculation" against heart disease

This evaluation gives the individual an excellent assessment of his fitness and cardiovascular risk. It also shows clearly where he may have problems in the future. He can then consult his physician to learn how these factors can be improved or controlled. In fact, we provide each participant with a duplicate copy of his printout, recommending that he pass it along to his physician.

---

* Behavior type; uric acid; weight; physical activity levels; cardio-respiratory fitness (physical condition).

130

The need for this type of testing stems from the fact that coronary heart disease gives no early-warning signals. The tragedy in heart disease is that it's swift, sudden and unannounced. All the individual can do is understand the risk factors, monitor them regularly, and maintain them at recommended values.

Every manager, especially after 40, should know the coronary risk he's running. He should be aware of, and in control of, the principal factors contributing to that risk. This, we can state flatly, is the best "inoculation" against coronary heart disease.

The company's involvement

There are some rules, of course, that should be followed in conducting such an evaluation. First of all, this type of testing must be voluntary. A corporation can make this testing available, but shouldn't insist on such examinations. Furthermore, the testing must be medically supervised and conducted with the approval of the participant's personal physician.

In addition, the results and conclusions must be confidential, provided only to the individual participant. But this doesn't mean that aggregated or group data can't be compiled for top management.

In fact, the availability of this group data in computerized form suggests a very intriguing possibility in the area of human-resource accounting.

Such group data would be a statement on organization health. Monitored over time, the information might bring to light the human effects of corporate change—the impact of new policies, procedures, structures.

Furthermore, the company might compare different levels of management, managers in different geographic locations and in different functional areas. The top echelons could also monitor conditions such as rapid growth and the threat of bankruptcy to detect possible changes in managers' health.

Interestingly, changes in managers' health might be used as one indicator of corporate problems. No one really knows whether the correlation would work in practice, but the very idea of being able to pinpoint the human cost of corporate change is challenging.

On the other hand, the greatest advantage of this testing is, of course, the possibility of intervening in the illness process before the results become catastrophic. And the corporation can play a number of roles in this intervention, ranging from simple encouragement to the provision of fitness programs and even exercise facilities for employees.

However, we emphasize again that the individual must accept the primary responsibility for coping with change and its stressful effects on his mind and body.

If your company doesn't have any form of human-resource accounting, or any kind of program to encourage fitness and good health habits, you can and should discuss the matter with senior management. Explain the facts as you've read them in these pages. Take the initiative with the organization—as with yourself.

What else you can do

To cope effectively with change as a stress-producing force, in addition to the steps outlined earlier in this chapter you may have to do a complete reassessment of your own attitudes and lifestyle. Research has shown that some individuals are more change-prone, and they're less efficient in dealing with stress resulting from change. But the individual does have some choice.

To become an effective manager of stress, you must maintain change events within tolerable limits. This isn't to say that you should suppress change, because change constitutes the dynamics of life itself. Instead, you *can* consciously plan those events that are controllable, so as to keep a firm grasp on the activities of day-to-day living.

At the same time, the manager who's aware that the unexpected does occur can prepare himself by retaining a reserve of energy to cope with unanticipated events.

People *can* make a conscious decision either to experience life as a series of inevitable and uncontrollable events, or to actively control and anticipate occurrences in the present and future. The two extremes in attitude may be termed "active participation" and "passive reaction," and the comparison opposite contrasts the types.

Styles of coping with change

Least effective	Most effective
(The passive reactor)	*(The active participator)*
1. Reacts passively to life's events.	1. Participates actively in his life.
2. Leaves his life to "fate." Tends to "cram" rather than "plan" his activites.	2. Maintains life change events within tolerable limits by making a conscious selection of controllable activities.
3. Little foresight or anticipation of events.	3. Anticipates and prepares for likely events in the foreseeable future. Has good foresight.
4. Allows events to accumulate until unable to cope when the unexpected arises.	4. Builds and maintains a reservoir of untapped time and energy to deal with unexpected events.
5. Perceives the environment, and most change events as generally threatening.	5. Views the environment objectively. Sorts events into categories of importance, urgency and degree of actual threat.
6. Faced with potentially stressful change, tends to react compulsively, most often in a stereotyped manner.	6. Faced with potentially stressful change, takes "time out" to evaluate alternative strategies, perhaps even adopting a novel solution to a novel problem.
7. May unconsciously choose a coping mechanism that actually increases resultant stress reaction through adverse consequences.	7. After careful evaluation, tries to adopt the mechanism of coping most apt to reduce potential stress and aid in successful adaptation.
8. Continues to tax his psycho-physiological capacity to the limit. Stress symptoms accumulate.	8. Stress is effectively eliminated or reduced. Continues to operate well within his adaptive range, and avoids over-taxing his psycho-physiological capacity.

The passive reactor

This individual tends to leave his life to fate. He prides himself on the number of activities and new undertakings he can cram into an already busy schedule. He doesn't anticipate the fact that sooner or later an unexpected event will occur that's too large to fit into his chaotic and overburdened lifestyle. Change, therefore, is not only more frequent (from a self-inflicted source), but, because it's often unanticipated, it hits harder.

The active participator

This individual simplifies his lifestyle by consciously selecting and timing the occurrences of specific milestones in his life. He's aware of his personal energy level (that is, his psychological and physical capacity), and doesn't judge personal success by the number of activities and new events he can handle without first breaking down or burning out. He leaves a reservoir of untapped time and energy for those unexpected events that otherwise may cause disruption and distress. In short, he's a "manager of change."

What can *you* do, right now, to begin your training in the management of stress?

The physician on our team, Dr. Rechnitzer, believes that the best possible mechanism for coping with stress is what he calls a sustaining passion.

If your sustaining passion is your vocation, then you can call it job satisfaction. And we know from our research that it's related to an absence of stress symptoms. The danger of a vocational sustaining passion is that it can end unexpectedly. There's always the possibility of enforced job change and illness —and, inevitably, retirement must come. Job satisfaction is healthful, but an *avocational* sustaining passion is a marvelous buttress and can be a saving substitute if the vocational satisfaction ends or collapses.

Ideally, the sustaining passion should be serious (as in five-year-olds at play), with a never-ending challenge, not to be dabbled in, having esthetic and spiritual components and not being dependent

134

on the availability of others.

Dr. Rechnitzer's greatest satisfaction as a physician has been to witness men recovering from their first brush with death who find a passion in themselves they didn't know existed, and to see it developed and nurtured. Because of his research, this has most often centered around the challenge and rewards of a highly trained and fit body and the awareness of something so basic. But he has also seen this consuming passion develop for wild life, orchids, theatre and the violin—and seen it to be equally effective.

These men have learned much about coping with stress, and the physician continues to learn from his patients.

In closing, we also suggest that you consider very carefully the following checklist of steps:

—Consciously assess your own pace of life at present. Take inventory of all recent changes, including current or upcoming change events. Analyze job situations, and identify those you find particularly stressful.

—Try to become aware of your own psycho-physiological threshold. Practise sensitivity in detecting stress symptoms— heart palpitations, headaches, rapid pulse, insomnia. Learn to identify a state of stress within yourself, so you can begin to deal with it directly.

—Simplify your life. Attempt to foresee the occurrence of specific stress-producing events on the job, and try to schedule them so they don't occur simultaneously. In the same way, budget change events in such a way that they remain within *your* perception of controllable limits. Don't suppress all change and tension—merely "manage" it.

—Leave job tensions at the office. Put your work life and your personal life in different compartments.

—Leave room within your coping range for unanticipated stress situations. Don't load your time and budget your energy to their absolute capacities. Maintain a state of readiness by staying healthy.

—When an unexpected stress situation or major change event arises, *stop* and think about it. Is it really as serious as it appears on the surface? Is it worth the expenditure of valuable energy resources in worrying and tension? Or, with the application of a little imagination and flexibility, can you adapt easily and readily?

—Evaluate the various alternative mechanisms at hand for coping with tension. Are the "old ways" still working effectively for you? Or is it time to take a break, get away from it all and evaluate new courses of action objectively?

—Begin to design and apply a broad repertoire of alternate responses. Be flexible and imaginative, and shy away from stereotyped reactions. Follow through by analyzing the implications and the range of consequences of your responses.

—Above all, be in conscious control of your life. Be an active participator, and a flexible one. Remember that, as a manger, you're particularly exposed to tension and very susceptible to stress.

—Remember, too, that stress isn't all bad. Some stress is both necessary and desirable in your life. The basic issue isn't its elimination but its containment and allocation—the management of stress.